Macmillan McGraw-Hill

California Mathematics

Concepts, Skills, and Problem Solving

2

Volume 2

Authors

Altieri • Balka • Day • Gonsalves • Grace • Krulik
Malloy • Molix-Bailey • Moseley • Mowry • Myren
Price • Reynosa • Santa Cruz • Silbey • Vielhaber

McGraw Hill Macmillan McGraw-Hill

About the Cover

California Focus How tall are you? Not nearly as tall as California Redwoods! The Coast Redwoods average 300–350 feet (91–107 meters) in height, yet their roots are only about 10 feet deep. Instead of growing deep, the roots spread out 250 feet (75 meters) from the tree trunk. No wonder the California Redwood is the State Tree of California.

Mathematics Focus: Measurement is an important topic in Second Grade. On the cover, a California Grizzly Bear is measuring the height of her cub. What other measurements can the students find on the cover?

The McGraw·Hill Companies

Send all inquiries to:
Macmillan/McGraw-Hill
8787 Orion Place
Columbus, OH 43240-4027

Volume 2
ISBN: 978-0-02-105706-1
MHID: 0-02-105706-0

Printed in the United States of America.

10 11 12 13   RMN/LEH   16 15 14 13

Contents in Brief

Mary Behr Altieri
Putnam/Northern
    Westchester BOCES
Yorktown Heights,
    New York

Don S. Balka
Professor Emeritus
Saint Mary's College
Notre Dame, Indiana

Roger Day, Ph.D.
Mathematics Department Chair
Pontiac Township High School
Pontiac, Illinois

Philip D. Gonsalves
Mathematics Coordinator
Alameda County Office
    of Education and
    California State
    University East Bay
Hayward, California

Ellen C. Grace
Consultant
Albuquerque,
    New Mexico

Stephen Krulik
Professor Emeritus
Mathematics Education
Temple University
Cherry Hill, New Jersey

Carol E. Malloy
Assistant Professor of
    Mathematics Education
University of North
    Carolina at Chapel Hill
Chapel Hill, North
    Carolina

Rhonda J. Molix-Bailey
Mathematics Consultant
Mathematics by Design
Desoto, Texas

Lois Gordon Moseley
Staff Developer
NUMBERS: Mathematics
    Professional
    Development
Houston, Texas

Brian Mowry
Independent Math Educational
    Consultant/Part-Time Pre-K
    Instructional Specialist
Austin Independent School District
Austin, Texas

Math Online Meet the Authors at ca.gr2math.com

Christina L. Myren
Consultant Teacher
Conejo Valley Unified
School District
Thousand Oaks, California

Jack Price
Professor Emeritus
California State
Polytechnic University
Pomona, California

Mary Esther Reynosa
Instructional Specialist for
Elementary Mathematics
Northside Independent
School District
San Antonio, Texas

Rafaela M. Santa Cruz
SDSU/CGU Doctoral
Program in Education
San Diego State University
San Diego, California

Robyn Silbey
Math Content Coach
Montgomery County
Public Schools
Gaithersburg, Maryland

Kathleen Vielhaber
Mathematics Consultant
St. Louis, Missouri

Contributing Authors

Viken Hovsepian
Professor of Mathematics
Rio Hondo College
Whittier, California

Donna J. Long
Mathematics Consultant
Indianapolis, Indiana

FOLDABLES **Dinah Zike**
Educational Consultant
Dinah-Might Activities, Inc.
San Antonio, Texas

Macmillian/McGraw-Hill wishes to thank the following professionals for their invaluable feedback during the development of the program. They reviewed a variety of instructional materials at different stages of development.

Cheryl L. Avalos
Mathematics Consultant
Hacienda Heights, California

William M. Bokesch
Rancho Bernardo High
   School
San Diego, California

Patty Brown
Teacher
John Muir Elementary
Fresno, California

David J. Chamberlain
Secondary Mathematics
   Resource Teacher
Capistrano Unified School
   District
San Juan Capistrano, California

Eppie Chung
K-6 Teacher
Modesto City Schools
Modesto, California

Lisa Marie Cirrincione
Middle School Teacher
Lincoln Middle School
Oceanside, California

Carol Cronk
Mathematics Program
   Specialist
San Bernardino City Unified
   School District
San Bernardino, California

Ilene Foster
Teacher Specialist–
   Mathematics
Pomona Unified School
   District
Pomona, California

Grant A. Fraser, Ph. D.
Professor of Mathematics
California State University,
   Los Angeles
Los Angeles, California

Suzanne Bocskai Freire
Teacher
Kingswood Elementary
Citrus Heights, California

Beth Holguin
Teacher
Graystone Elementary
San Jose, California

Donna M. Kopenski, Ed. D.
Mathematics Coordinator K-5
City Heights Educational
　Collaborative
San Diego, California

Kelly Mack
6th Grade Teacher
Captain Jason Dahl
　Elementary
San Jose, California

Juvenal Martinez
Dual Immersion/ESL
　Instructor
Aeolian Elementary
Whittier, California

John McGuire
Associate Principal
Pacific Union School
Arcata, California

Dr. Donald R. Price
Teacher, Adjunct Professor
Rowland Unified School
　District
Rowland Heights, California

Kasey St. James
Mathematics Teacher
Sunny Hills High School
Fullerton, California

Arthur K. Wayman, Ph. D.
Professor of Mathematics
　Emeritus
California State University,
　Long Beach
Long Beach, California

Beverly Wells
First Grade Teacher
Mineral King Elementary
　School
Visalia, California

Frances Basich Whitney
Project Director, Mathematics
　K-12
Santa Cruz County Office of
　Education
Capitola, California

Consultants

Macmillan/McGraw-Hill wishes to thank the following professionals for their feedback. They were instrumental in providing valuable input toward the development of this program in these specific areas.

Mathematical Content

Viken Hovsepian
Professor of Mathematics
Rio Hondo College
Whittier, California

Grant A. Fraser, Ph.D.
Professor of Mathematics
California State University, Los Angeles
Los Angeles, California

Arthur K. Wayman, Ph.D.
Professor of Mathematics Emeritus
California State University, Long Beach
Long Beach, California

Assessment

Jane D. Gawronski
Director of Assessment and Outreach
San Diego State University
San Diego, California

Cognitive Guided Instruction

Susan B. Empson
Associate Professor of Mathematics
   and Science Education
University of Texas at Austin
Austin, Texas

English Learners

Cheryl Avalos
Mathematics Consultant
Los Angeles County Office of Education, Retired
Hacienda Heights, California

Kathryn Heinze
Graduate School of Education
Hamline University
St. Paul, Minnesota

Family Involvement

Paul Giganti, Jr.
Mathematics Education Consultant
Albany, California

Literature

David M. Schwartz
Children's Author, Speaker, Storyteller
Oakland, California

Vertical Alignment

Berchie Holliday
National Educational Consultant
Silver Spring, Maryland

Deborah A. Hutchens, Ed.D.
Principal
Norfolk Highlands Elementary
Chesapeake, Virginia

viii

California Reviewers

Each California Reviewer reviewed at least two chapters of the Student Edition, giving feedback and suggestions for improving the effectiveness of the mathematics instruction.

Sherry G. Anderson
Teacher/G.A.T.E. Coordinator
Will Rogers Elementary
Lynwood, California

Ysaaca Axelrod
Kindergarten Teacher
El Monte Elementary
Concord, California

Cathy Bullock
Teacher
Capri Elementary
Encinitas, California

Michelle Callender
Teacher
Morgan/Kincaid Preparatory School
   of Integrated Studies
Victorville, California

M. Olivia Campos
4th Grade Teacher
Morrison Elementary
Norwalk, California

Malaura Page Easton, M.S.
Kindergarten Teacher
La Pluma School
La Mirada, California

Priscilla S. Edwards
5th Grade Classroom Teacher
David Reese Elementary
Sacramento, California

Lisa B. Friedberg
4th Grade Teacher
Alderwood Basics Plus School
Irvine, California

Wendy Smith Hernandez
Kindergarten Teacher
Herndon-Barstow Elementary
Fresno, California

Beth Holguin
Teacher
Graystone School
San Jose, California

Kristi Iverson
First Grade Teacher
Village Oaks Elementary
Stockton, California

Sheri Leiken
Teacher
Weathersfield Elementary
Thousand Oaks, California

Sarab H. Lopes
Teacher
Anza Elementary
El Cajon, California

Karen E. Lund
5th Grade Teacher
Meadow Park Elementary
Irvine, California

Efrain Melendez
Teacher
Livermore Valley USD
Livermore, California

Jean A. Nelson
Teacher
Fremont Elementary School
Alhambra, California

Tara Pahia
Elementary Teacher
Bear Gulch Elementary
Rancho Cucamonga, California

Dr. Donald R. Price
Teacher, Adjunct Professor
Rowland Unified School District
Rowland Heights, California

Kitty Ritz, M.A.
Teacher
Monte Vista Elementary
Rohnert Park, California

Corinne E. Schwartz
First Grade Teacher
Lincrest Elementary School
Yuba City, California

Deborah Shapiro
5th Grade Teacher
Nancy Cory
Lancaster, California

Maureen Smith
Curriculum Specialist
Fremont Unified School Dist.
   (retired 6/2006)
Fremont, California

Joseph M. Snodgrass
3rd Grade Teacher
Park Elementary School
Alhambra, California

Marie W. Stevens
Elementary Mathematics
   Coordinator
LAUSD
Los Angeles, California

Jane Traut
Classroom Teacher
Lang Ranch Elementary School
Thousand Oaks, California

Rachel C. Trowbridge
Teacher
Evergreen Elementary
San Jose, California

Cynthia H. Vandemoortel
Educator
Alderwood Basics Plus School
Irvine, California

Norine Yale
Teacher
Justin Elementary
Simi Valley, California

Dr. Darlene York
Education Consultant
Associate Professor
Antioch University
Seattle, Washington

Contents

Start Smart

Contents

= Hands-On Activity

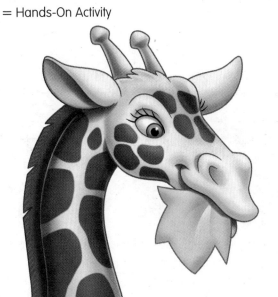

H.O.T. Problems
Higher Order Thinking 26, 28

Problem Solving 20, 34, 38, 42

WRITING IN ►MATH 22

Contents

H.O.T. Problems
Higher Order Thinking 54, 68

Problem Solving 60, 64

WRITING IN ▶MATH 56

Contents

 = Hands-On Activity

H.O.T. Problems
Higher Order Thinking 86, 98, 100

Problem Solving 94

WRITING IN ▶ MATH 84

Contents

H.O.T. Problems
Higher Order Thinking 134

Problem Solving 114, 130

WRITING IN ►MATH 118

xiv

Contents

 = Hands-On Activity

H.O.T. Problems
Higher Order Thinking 158

Problem Solving 148, 150, 160, 164

WRITING IN ▸ MATH 154

Copyright © Macmillan/McGraw-Hill, a division of The McGraw-Hill Companies, Inc.

Contents

Contents

= Hands-On Activity

H.O.T. Problems
Higher Order Thinking 214, 230

Problem **S**olving 212, 216, 234, 236

WRITING IN ►MATH 226

Copyright © Macmillan/McGraw-Hill, a division of The McGraw-Hill Companies, Inc.

Contents

H.O.T. Problems
Higher Order Thinking 270

Problem Solving 250, 252, 254, 260, 268

WRITING IN ▶MATH 274

Contents

 = Hands-On Activity

H.O.T. Problems
Higher Order Thinking 288, 300

Problem Solving 296, 302

WRITING IN ▶MATH 286

Contents

Contents

 = Hands-On Activity

H.O.T. Problems
Higher Order Thinking 354, 362

Problem Solving 348, 360

WRITING IN ▶MATH 350

Copyright © Macmillan/McGraw-Hill, a division of The McGraw-Hill Companies, Inc.

xxi

Contents

H.O.T. Problems
Higher Order Thinking 390, 394

Problem Solving 378, 380, 388, 402

WRITING IN ►MATH 382

CHAPTER 13

Three-Digit Addition

 = Hands-On Activity

H.O.T. Problems
Higher Order Thinking 416

Problem Solving 414, 428

WRITING IN ►MATH 426

Copyright © Macmillan/McGraw-Hill, a division of The McGraw-Hill Companies, Inc.

Contents

H.O.T. Problems
Higher Order Thinking 442, 444

Problem Solving 456

WRITING IN ▶MATH 454

Contents

California Standards Review

Looking Ahead to the Grade 3 Standards

H.O.T. Problems
Higher Order Thinking 476, 478

Problem Solving 468, 470, 474

WRITING IN ▶ MATH 472

Contents

Student Handbook

Reference

CHAPTER 9

Fractions

Key Vocabulary
- fraction
- equal parts
- whole
- unit fraction
- group

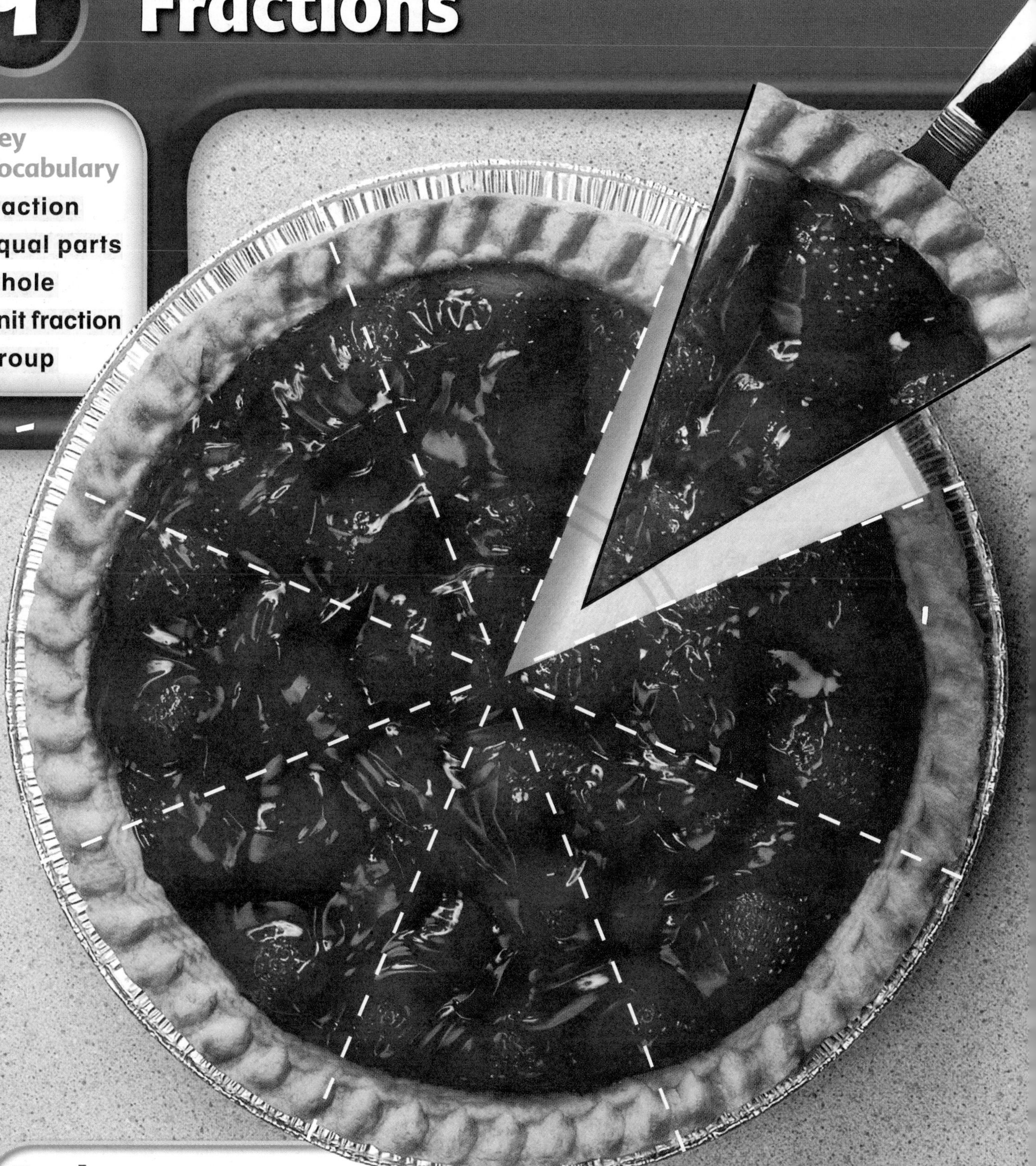

Explore

How many equal parts do you see in this pie?

_____ equal parts

Name _____

Are You Ready for Chapter 9?

Write the number of parts.

1.

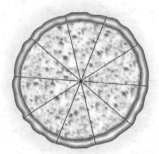

_____ pizza slices

2.

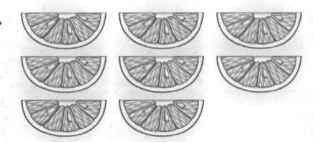

_____ orange slices

Circle the shapes that are the same size.

3.

4.

5. Marcia baked a cherry pie. She needs to share the pie with 4 people. Draw lines in the pie so that everyone gets a share of pie that is the same size.

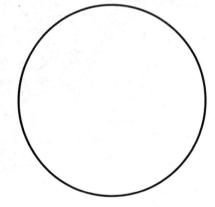

This page checks skills needed for Chapter 9.

MATH at HOME

Dear Family,

Today my class started Chapter 9, **Fractions**. In this chapter, I will learn about fractions from $\frac{1}{2}$ to $\frac{1}{12}$. Here is an activity we can do and a list of books we can read together.

Love, _____

Activity

Have your child look around the house to find objects that show equal parts. Count how many equal parts there are.

Key Vocabulary

fraction a number that represents part of a whole or part of a set

equal parts each part is the same size

Math Online Click on the eGlossary link at ca.gr2math.com to find out more about these words. There are 13 languages.

Books to Read

Fraction Action
by Loreen Leedy
Holiday House,
1996.

Apple Fractions
by Jerry Pallotta
Cartwheel,
2003.

Fraction Fun
by David A. Adler
Holiday House,
1997.

Estimada familia:

Hoy mi clase comenzó el Capítulo 9, **Las fracciones**. En este capítulo, aprenderé sobre fracciones desde $\frac{1}{2}$ hasta $\frac{1}{12}$. A continuación, hay una actividad que podemos hacer y una lista de libros que podemos leer juntos.

Cariños,

_____

Actividad

Pídale a su hijo(a) que busque por la casa objetos que muestren partes iguales. Cuenten cuántas partes iguales hay.

Vocabulario clave

fracción número que representa parte de un todo o parte de un conjunto

partes iguales cada parte es del mismo tamaño

Math Online Visiten el enlace eGlossary en ca.gr2math.com para averiguar más sobre estas palabras, las cuales se muestran en 13 idiomas.

Libros recomendados

¡Aomer fracciones!
de Bruce Mcmillan
Lectorum Publications, Inc., 1991.

Partes de un entero
de Linda Trumbauer
Red Brick, 2006.

¿De cuantas maneras se puede cortar un pastel?
de Jane Belk Moncure
Childs World, 1994.

Name _____

Other Fractions

Get Ready

Main Idea

I will make and identify more than one equal part of a whole.

These fractions name more than one equal part of the whole.

Three-fourths is yellow.

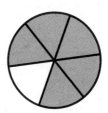

Five-sixths is orange.

3 of 4 parts are yellow.

$$\frac{3 \text{ yellow parts}}{4 \text{ total parts}} \rightarrow \frac{3}{4}$$

5 of 6 parts are orange.

$$\frac{5 \text{ orange parts}}{6 \text{ total parts}} \rightarrow \frac{5}{6}$$

Check

Use fraction circles to build each fraction.
Write the fraction.

1.

2. 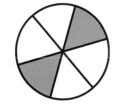 ___

3. 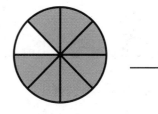 ___

Color to show the fraction.

4. $\frac{2}{3}$

5. $\frac{4}{7}$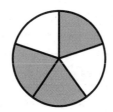

6. $\frac{7}{10}$

7. **Talk About It** What does the top number of a fraction tell you? What does the bottom number of a fraction tell you?

Use fraction circles to build each fraction.
Write the fraction.

8.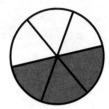

_____

9.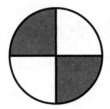

_____

10.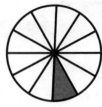

_____

Color to show the fraction.

11. $\frac{2}{4}$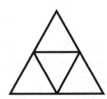

12. $\frac{3}{8}$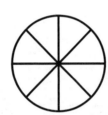

13. $\frac{2}{10}$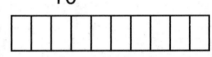

14. $\frac{7}{8}$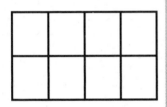

15. $\frac{2}{5}$

16. $\frac{3}{9}$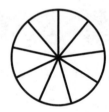

H.O.T. Problem

Thinking Math

17. Look at each fraction.

$\frac{1}{4}$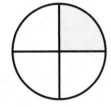

$\frac{2}{8}$

How are they alike?

_____

_____

Math at Home Activity: Draw a shape and divide it into 8 equal parts. Ask your child to show you $\frac{3}{8}$.

Name _____

Problem-Solving Strategy
Draw a Picture

Main Idea

I will draw a picture to solve problems.

Ted ate one part of an orange. The orange had twelve equal parts.

What fraction of the orange did he eat?

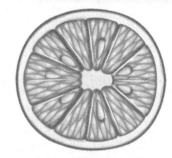

Understand

What do I know? Underline what you know.
What do I need to find out? Circle the question.

Plan

How will I solve the problem?
I will draw a picture to find the fraction.

Solve

Draw a picture.

> **Remember**
> Divide your drawing into 12 parts.

Ted ate _____ of the orange.

Check

Look Back
Does my answer make sense?

Copyright © Macmillan/McGraw-Hill, a division of The McGraw-Hill Companies, Inc.

Try It

Draw a picture to solve.

1. Steve cuts a pizza into 6 equal pieces.
   He eats $\frac{2}{6}$ of the pizza. How many pieces of
   pizza are left?

_____ pieces

2. There are 8 equal parts of a sandwich. Diego
   eats three of those pieces. What fraction of
   the sandwich does he eat?

_____ of the sandwich

Your Turn

Draw a picture to solve.

3. Troy's bagel is cut into 4 equal pieces.
   Three pieces have strawberry jelly on top.
   What fraction of the bagel has no jelly?

_____ bagel

4. Carla's garden has 5 equal parts. She
   planted beans and corn. She planted beans
   in 2 parts. What fraction of the garden did
   Carla plant in corn?

_____ of the garden

Copyright © Macmillan/McGraw-Hill, a division of The McGraw-Hill Companies, Inc.

Math at Home Activity: Have your child explain the picture he or she drew to solve the problem in Exercise 4.

Name _____

Fractions Equal to 1

Main Idea

I will write a fraction to show a whole.

You can write a fraction for the whole.

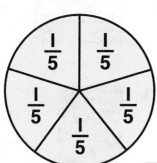

There are 5 yellow parts.
There are 5 total parts.

$$\frac{5 \text{ yellow parts} \longrightarrow}{5 \text{ total parts} \longrightarrow} \quad \frac{5}{5}$$

The fraction for the whole is $\dfrac{5}{5}$.

There are 5 pieces of pie. No pieces have been eaten. I have $\frac{5}{5}$. I have one whole pie.

The fraction for the whole always

equals 1. $\dfrac{5}{5} = \dfrac{1}{\rule{1.5cm}{0.4pt}}$

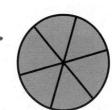

Check

Count the parts. Write the fraction.
Circle the fractions that equal 1.

1. 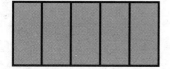 _____

2. _____

3. _____

4. 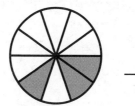 _____

5. **Talk About It** Why does a fraction for a whole have the same number on the top and the bottom?

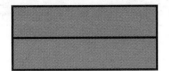
Count the parts. Write the fraction.
Circle the fractions that equal 1.

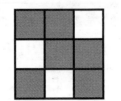

Remember
Write the number of colored parts on top. Write the total number of equal parts on the bottom.

6. 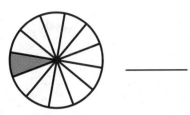 _____

7. 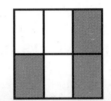 _____

8. 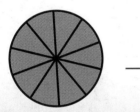 _____

9. 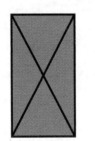 _____

10. _____ (circle, colored)

11. _____

Data File

Half Dome is a huge rock landform in Yosemite National Park. It is half of what was once a giant rock dome. The missing half fell off a long, long time ago.

12. Circle the fraction that shows the part that is left.

 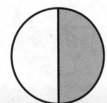  

Math at Home Activity: Cut a sandwich or pizza into equal parts. Ask your child to name the fraction for the whole.

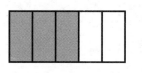
Name _____

Write the fraction for the colored part.

1.

2.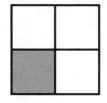

3.

Color to show the fraction.

4. $\dfrac{1}{7}$

5. $\dfrac{2}{3}$

6. $\dfrac{3}{4}$

Write the fraction. Circle the fractions that equal 1.

7.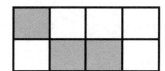

8.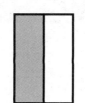

9.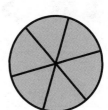

_____   _____   _____

10. 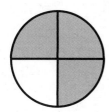 ___ — ___

11.  ___ — ___

12.  ___ — ___

13. Tia cut a sandwich into 4 equal pieces.
Draw the lines on the sandwich. Write the fraction.

_____

Spiral Review   Chapters 1–9

Complete the fact family.

14. $3 + 9 =$ _____ $12 - 3 =$ _____

   $9 + 3 =$ _____ $12 - 9 =$ _____

Subtract.

15. 76¢
      − 12¢

16. 44¢
      − 38¢

17. 35¢
      − 27¢

18. 68¢
      − 19¢

Multiply.

19. $6 \times 10 =$ _____   **20.** $5 \times 7 =$ _____   **21.** $2 \times 3 =$ _____

Subtract. Then divide.

22.

$18 -$ _____ $-$ _____ $-$ _____ $-$ _____ $-$ _____ $-$ _____ $=$ _____

$18 \div 3 =$ _____

Find the total using skip-counting.

23. Ken put toy cars into 5 groups of 4.
     How many toy cars does he have?

   _____ toy cars

Formative Assessment

Compare Fractions

Get Ready

Main Idea

I will compare unit fractions.

You can compare unit fractions using greater than > or less than <.

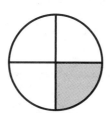

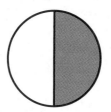

$\frac{1}{4}$ is colored.

$\frac{1}{2}$ is colored.

$\frac{1}{4}$ is less than $\frac{1}{2}$.

$\frac{1}{2}$ is greater than $\frac{1}{4}$.

$\frac{1}{4}$ $\bigcirc$< $\frac{1}{2}$

$\frac{1}{2}$ $\bigcirc$> $\frac{1}{4}$

✓ Check

Use fraction circles to build each fraction.
Compare the colored parts. Write < or >.

1.

$\frac{1}{4}$ $\bigcirc$ $\frac{1}{8}$

2.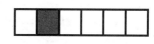

$\frac{1}{6}$ $\bigcirc$ $\frac{1}{12}$

3.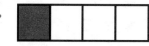

$\frac{1}{3}$ $\bigcirc$ $\frac{1}{6}$

4.

$\frac{1}{5}$ $\bigcirc$ $\frac{1}{6}$

5. **Talk About It** Is $\frac{1}{8} < \frac{1}{10}$? Explain.

> **Remember**
> \> is greater than and < is less than.

Use fraction circles to build each fraction.
Compare the shaded parts. Write < or >.

6.

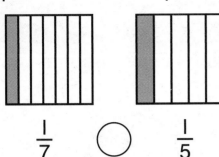

$\frac{1}{7}$ ◯ $\frac{1}{5}$

7.

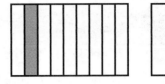

$\frac{1}{9}$ $\frac{1}{5}$

8.

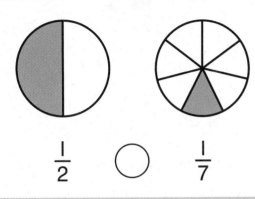

$\frac{1}{2}$ ◯ $\frac{1}{7}$

9.

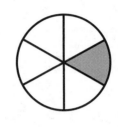

$\frac{1}{6}$ $\frac{1}{8}$

Compare the fractions. Write < or >.
You may draw a picture.

10. $\frac{1}{2}$ ◯ $\frac{1}{3}$

11. $\frac{1}{10}$ ◯ $\frac{1}{5}$

12. $\frac{1}{3}$ ◯ $\frac{1}{4}$

13. $\frac{1}{3}$ ◯ $\frac{1}{8}$

14. $\frac{1}{5}$ ◯ $\frac{1}{4}$

15. $\frac{1}{12}$ ◯ $\frac{1}{6}$

Problem Solving

Visual Thinking Circle the fraction that matches the statement.

16. is greater than $\frac{1}{2}$

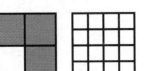

17. is less than $\frac{1}{2}$

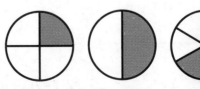

Math at Home Activity: Fold a piece of paper into 4 equal parts. Fold another piece in half. Ask your child what fraction each shows. Have your child tell you which fraction is less.

Name _____

Circle the fraction that tells how much of each pie has been eaten.

1. $\dfrac{1}{12}$ $\dfrac{1}{3}$ $\dfrac{1}{2}$ $\dfrac{1}{8}$

2. $\dfrac{1}{12}$ $\dfrac{1}{3}$ $\dfrac{1}{2}$ $\dfrac{1}{8}$

3. $\dfrac{1}{12}$ $\dfrac{1}{3}$ $\dfrac{1}{2}$ $\dfrac{1}{4}$

4. $\dfrac{1}{12}$ $\dfrac{1}{3}$ $\dfrac{1}{2}$ $\dfrac{1}{8}$

5. $\dfrac{1}{3}$ $\dfrac{1}{8}$ $\dfrac{1}{2}$ $\dfrac{1}{12}$

Fraction Puzzles

Understand Fractions

You Will Need

- cubes

Play with a partner:
- Roll a [1] or [6].
- Move to that number.
- Show the fraction with your cubes.
- If you are right, put your ⚫⚪ on the number.
- When all the numbers are covered, the player with more counters wins.

Name _____

Unit Fractions of a Group

Main Idea

I will write fractions to show one part of a group.

Vocabulary

group

A fraction can name one equal part of a **group**.

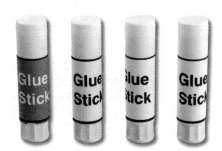

The top number tells how many equal parts you are talking about. The bottom number tells how many total parts are in the group.

1 of 4 equal parts are blue.
One-fourth is blue.

$$\frac{1 \text{ blue part}}{4 \text{ total parts}} \longrightarrow \frac{1}{4}$$

Check

Write the fraction for the yellow part of the group.

1.

$\dfrac{1 \text{ yellow part}}{5 \text{ total parts}}$

2.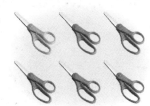

$\dfrac{\square \text{ yellow part}}{\square \text{ total parts}}$

3.

$\dfrac{\square \text{ yellow part}}{\square \text{ total parts}}$

4.

$\dfrac{\square \text{ yellow part}}{\square \text{ total parts}}$

5. **Talk About It** What does the fraction $\frac{1}{4}$ of a group mean?

Practice

Write the fraction for the red part of the group.

6.

_____ are red

7.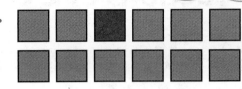

_____ are red

8.

_____ are red

9.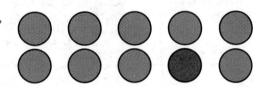

_____ are red

10.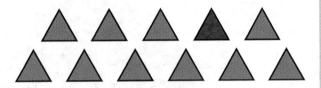

_____ are red

11.

_____ are red

H.O.T. Problems

Explaining Math

12. Circle the pictures or words that show the same fraction.

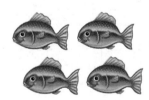      one fifth $\frac{1}{5}$

13. How did you know which pictures or words show the same fraction?

_____

_____

Math at Home Activity: Make groups of white socks and 1 black sock. Ask your child to tell what fraction of the group shows black.

Name _____

Other Fractions of a Group

Main Idea

I will identify fractions of more than one part of a group.

A fraction can name more than one part of a group.

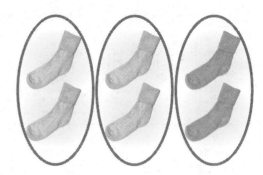

There are 2 equal parts.
I of the 2 parts is yellow.

The yellow part is $\frac{1}{2}$ of 4 buttons.

There are 3 equal parts.
2 of the 3 parts are yellow.

The yellow part is $\frac{2}{3}$ of 6 socks.

Check

Write the fraction for the orange part.

1.

$\frac{}{}$ of 8 shorts

2.
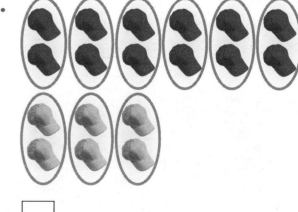

$\frac{}{}$ of 18 caps

3. **Talk About It** How would you draw a picture to show $\frac{2}{3}$ of 15 baseballs?

Write the fraction for the yellow part.

4.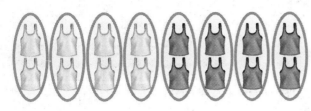

$\boxed{} \over \boxed{}$ of 16 shirts

5.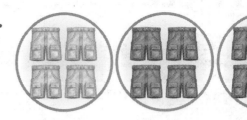

$\boxed{} \over \boxed{}$ of 12 shorts

6.

$\boxed{} \over \boxed{}$ of 10 shoes

7.

$\boxed{} \over \boxed{}$ of 4 sweat shirts

Problem Solving

8. Number Sense What fraction of the stickers are tigers? Explain how you found your answer.

$\boxed{} \over \boxed{}$ of 8 stickers are tigers

_____

_____

_____

_____

_____

Math at Home Activity: Ask your child to divide a group of pennies into $\frac{1}{2}$, $\frac{1}{3}$, and $\frac{1}{4}$.

Problem-Solving Investigation

Main Idea

I will choose a strategy to solve the problem.

Your Mission:
Find what fraction of the fish Jerry caught.

My dad and I went fishing. We caught 12 fish. I caught 3 of the fish. What fraction of the fish did I catch?

Understand

What do I know? Underline what you know.
What do I need to find out? Circle it.

Plan

How will I solve the problem?
One way is to draw a picture.

Solve

Draw a picture.

Remember
Start with 12 fish.

Jerry caught _____ of the fish.

Check

Look Back
Does my answer make sense?

Mixed Problem Solving

Choose a strategy. Solve.

Problem-Solving Strategies

- Draw a picture
- Logical reasoning
- Act it out

1. There were 16 people at the park. 4 were on the swings. What fraction of the people were on the swings?

_____

2. Jim's mom cut a watermelon in half. Jim and his sister shared one of the halves equally. His mom and dad shared the other half. How much of the watermelon did Jim eat?

_____

3. There were 7 birds in the tree. 3 of the birds were robins, and the others were blue jays. What fraction of the birds were blue jays?

_____

4. These are Erin's buttons.

What fraction of the buttons are yellow?   _____ are yellow

Math at Home Activity: Take advantage of problem-solving opportunities during daily routines such as riding in the car, bedtime, putting away groceries, planning schedules, and so on.

I take care of my fish. I feed them, and I make sure their home is clean.

Fish need care just like dogs and cats!

FOLD DOWN

D

Problem Solving
in Science

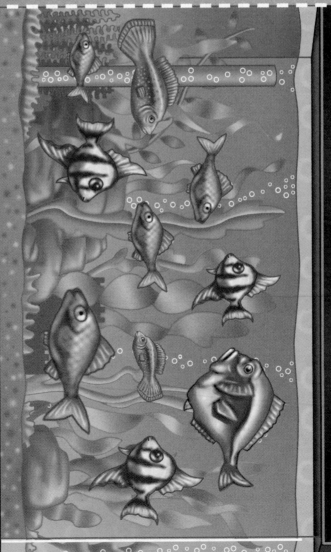

Real-World MATH

I have ten fish in my tank. There are many places for my fish to hide.

This book belongs to

_____

A

Four of my fish are almost always behind the plants. That means I can only see six fish at a time.

What fraction of my fish can I see?

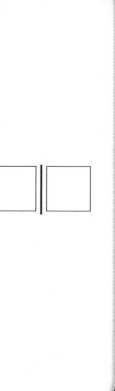

Wait and watch closely! Two of my fish are hiding. Now I can see eight of my fish.

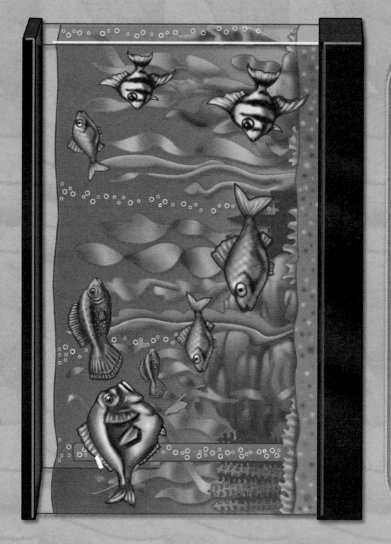

What fraction of my fish are still hiding?

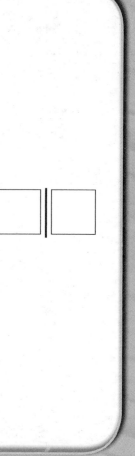

Name _____

Vocabulary

Circle the word that best completes the sentence.

1. Use a fraction to name _____ .

   units   numbers   equal parts

2. A _____ is made up of equal parts.   fraction   whole   unit

Concepts

Write the fraction for the colored part.

3. 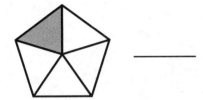 _____

4. 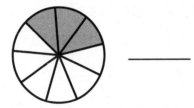 _____

5. 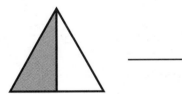 _____

6. 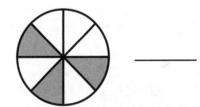 _____

Color to show the fraction.

7. $\frac{1}{2}$

8. $\frac{7}{8}$

Write the fraction. Circle the fractions that equal 1.

9. 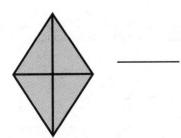 _____

10. 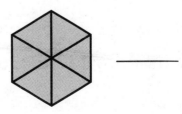 _____

Compare the fractions. Write < or >.

11.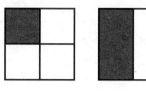

$$\frac{1}{4} \bigcirc \frac{1}{2}$$

12.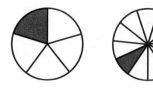

$$\frac{1}{5} \bigcirc \frac{1}{11}$$

13. Write a fraction for the purple part of the group.

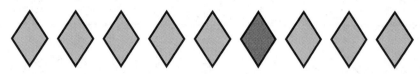

_____

14. What fraction of the group of stickers are heart stickers?

_____

15. Write the fraction for the blue parts.

_____ of 10 mittens

Problem Solving

16. A pizza has 8 slices. How many slices would you color to show that the whole pizza has been eaten?

_____ slices

17. Is $\frac{7}{8} > \frac{1}{8}$ true or false? Explain.

_____

308   three hundred eight

Name _____

Listen as your teacher reads each problem.
Choose the correct answer.

A Look at the fraction bars. Which fraction bar shows one-eighth colored?

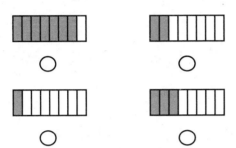

○   ○

○   ○

B What fraction of the group of shapes is hearts?

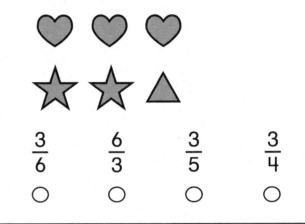

$\dfrac{3}{6}$ $\dfrac{6}{3}$ $\dfrac{3}{5}$ $\dfrac{3}{4}$

○   ○   ○   ○

Listen as your teacher reads each problem.
Choose the correct answer.

1 What fraction of this shape is colored?

$\dfrac{1}{3}$ $\dfrac{2}{3}$ $\dfrac{3}{3}$ $\dfrac{3}{2}$

○   ○   ○   ○

3 Which fraction is equal to one whole?

$\dfrac{1}{4}$ $\dfrac{8}{8}$ $\dfrac{5}{8}$ $\dfrac{1}{2}$

○   ○   ○   ○

2 Look at the group of circles. What fraction names the colored part of the group?

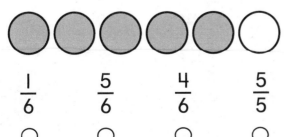

$\dfrac{1}{6}$ $\dfrac{5}{6}$ $\dfrac{4}{6}$ $\dfrac{5}{5}$

○   ○   ○   ○

4 Mrs. Wong divided the class into groups. Each group has one-fourth of all the students in the class. How many groups are there?

2   4   6   12

○   ○   ○   ○

5 Which of the following fractions is the greatest?

$\frac{1}{12}$ $\frac{1}{4}$ $\frac{1}{2}$ $\frac{1}{7}$
○   ○   ○   ○

8 What is the solution to this problem?

$$\begin{array}{r} 23 \\ +\ 8 \\ \hline \end{array}$$

33   31   29   28
○   ○   ○   ○

6 Sara has these coins. How much money is this?

78¢   89¢   95¢   98¢
○   ○   ○   ○

9 Beth ate one-half of her sandwich. Karen ate one-fourth of her sandwich. Which fraction shows the greatest amount that was eaten?

$\frac{1}{10}$ $\frac{1}{4}$ $\frac{1}{5}$ $\frac{1}{2}$
○   ○   ○   ○

7 Bart has forty-three bottle tops. Frank has twenty-nine bottle tops. About how many more bottle tops does Bart have?

10   20   40   70
○   ○   ○   ○

10 There are twelve cats at the farm. Each cat has four legs. How many cat legs are there altogether?

12   48   49   55
○   ○   ○   ○

STOP

310   three hundred ten

Summative Assessment

CHAPTER 10

Numbers to 1,000

Key Vocabulary

hundreds

expanded form

thousand

Explore

Look at all of the penguins. Would you estimate the number of penguins to be greater than 100? Circle it.

Yes   No

Name _____

Are You Ready for Chapter 10?

Write the numbers in order.

1. 13, 65, 8, 90 _____, _____, _____, _____

2. 100, 44, 23, 89 _____, _____, _____, _____

3. 35, 53, 92, 29 _____, _____, _____, _____

Write the number.

4. An 8 is in the tens place and a 3 is in the ones place. _____

5. A 7 is in the tens place and a 2 is in the ones place. _____

6. A 3 is in the tens place and a 0 is in the ones place. _____

Compare using <, >, or =.

7. 27 ◯ 36

8. 15 ◯ 15

9. 45 ◯ 29

10. 12 ◯ 20

11. Rosa skip-counts by twos to count the shoes in her closet. Show how she counts.

2, 4, _____, _____, _____

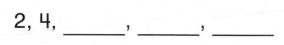

This page checks skills needed for Chapter 10.

Dear Family,

Today my class started Chapter 10, **Numbers to 1,000.** In this chapter, I will learn to compare and order numbers to 1,000. Here is an activity we can do and a list of books we can read together.

Love, _____

Activity

Visit your local library with your child. Write out 000–099, 100–199, 200–299, etc. up to 999 on separate pieces of paper. Walk through the non-fiction children's area and find the subject of the books within each range of numbers. Find an interesting book in each section and write down its name and number.

Key Vocabulary

expanded form the representation of a number as a sum that shows the value of each digit; Ex: 826 is 800 + 20 + 6

thousand a place value of a number

Math Online Click on the eGlossary link at ca.gr2math.com to find out more about these words. There are 13 languages.

Books to Read

Fun with 9umbers
by Massin
Creative Editions,
1995.

The History of Counting
by Denise Schmandt-
Besserat
HarperCollins, 1999.

How Much Is a Million?
by David M. Schwartz
HarperTrophy, 2004.

Estimada Familia:

Hoy mi clase comenzó el Capítulo 10, **Los números hasta 1,000.** En este capítulo, aprenderé a comparar y a ordenar números hasta 1,000. A continuación, hay una actividad que podemos hacer y una lista de libros que podemos leer juntos.

Cariños,

_____

Actividad

Visiten la biblioteca local con su hijo(a). En trozos de papel separados, escriban 000-099, 100-199, 200-299, etc. hasta 999. Caminen por la sección infantil de no ficción y busquen los temas de los libros dentro de cada rango de números. Busquen un libro interesante en cada sección y anoten su título y número

Vocabulario clave

forma desarrollada la representación de un número como una suma que muestra el valor de cada dígito; Ej.: 826 es 800 + 20 + 6

millares el valor de posición de un número

Math Online Visiten el enlace eGlossary en ca.gr2math.com para averiguar más sobre estas palabras, las cuales se muestran en 13 idiomas.

Libros recomendados

Cuanto es un millon?
de David M. Schwartz
Scholastic Inc., 1985.

¿Sabes contar hasta un googol?
de Robert E. Wells
Juventud, 2004.

El jarrón mágico. Una aventura matemática.
de Mitsumasa Anno
Juventud, 1993.

Name _____

Hundreds

Get Ready

Main Idea

I will write numbers as hundreds, tens, and ones.

Vocabulary

hundreds

Each plate holds 100.

I **hundred** = 10 tens = 100 ones

Check

Use base ten blocks to make groups of hundreds.
Write how many hundreds, tens, and ones.

1. _____ hundreds = _____ tens = _____ ones = _____

2.  _____ hundred = _____ tens = _____ ones = _____

3.  _____ hundreds = _____ tens = _____ ones = _____

4. **Talk About It** How many ones are in I hundred?
How do you know?

Use base ten blocks to make groups of hundreds.
Write how many hundreds, tens, and ones.

5.

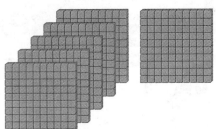

_____ hundreds = _____ tens = _____ ones = _____

6.

_____ hundreds = _____ tens = _____ ones = _____

7.

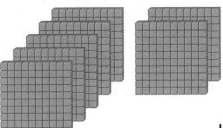

_____ hundreds = _____ tens = _____ ones = _____

8.

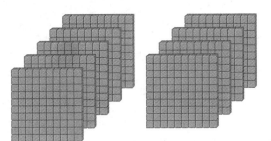

_____ hundreds = _____ tens = _____ ones = _____

9. **WRITING IN** ►**MATH** Explain how 20 tens is
the same as 200.

_____

_____

Math at Home Activity: Ask your child to count by hundreds to 900.

Name _____

Hundreds, Tens, and Ones

Get Ready

Main Idea

I will use hundreds, tens, and ones to show numbers.

There are 427 pennies in this jar. Use hundreds, tens, and ones to show 427.

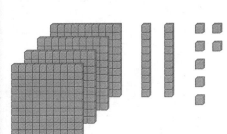

hundreds	tens	ones
4	2	7

4 2 7 four hundred twenty-seven.

Check

Use base ten blocks to show each number. Write how many hundreds, tens, and ones. Then write the number.

1. Show 2 , 6 |, and 3 ▪.

hundreds	tens	ones

_____

2. Show 5 , 1 |, and 8 ▪.

hundreds	tens	ones

_____

3. **Talk About It** What is the value of the 1 in 712, 165, and 381?

Use base ten blocks to show each number. Write how many hundreds, tens, and ones. Then write the number.

4. Show 3 , 8 , and 2 .

hundreds	tens	ones

_____

5. Show 6 , 4 , and 3 .

hundreds	tens	ones

_____

6. Show 7 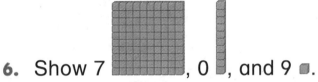, 0 , and 9 .

hundreds	tens	ones

_____

Data File

The Transamerica Pyramid is an office building in San Francisco. The building measures 853 feet high from base to top. It is 152 feet wide at the bottom, but only 45 feet wide at the top!

7. What number has an 8 in the hundreds place? _____

8. What number has a 5 in the ones place?

_____

Math at Home Activity: Write the number 647. Ask your child to tell you how many hundreds, tens, and ones.

Problem-Solving Strategy
Make a List

Main Idea

I will make a list to solve problems.

The number of Amanda's house is a 3-digit number. The sum of the digits is 6. The digits are all different. None of the digits is 0. How many different house numbers could there be?

Understand

What do I know? Underline what you know.

What do I need to find out? Circle the question.

Plan

How will I solve the problem?

I will make a list of all possible house numbers.

Solve

Make a list of the possible house numbers.

| 123 | 213 | 321 |
| 132 | 231 | 312 |

There are _____ possible house numbers.

Check

Look back.

Does my answer make sense?

Try It

Make a list to solve.

1. Mario, Kay, and Martin are sitting for a class picture. List all the ways they can sit.

_____

2. Loretta is putting the letters RES for Richardson Elementary School on the bulletin board. She forgot what order to put them in. How many different ways could she arrange the letters, RES?

   The letters can be arranged in _____ ways.

_____

Your Turn

Make a list to solve.

3. You are going to make a model of a dinosaur. There are red heads, red bodies, green heads, and green bodies. How many different models can you make?

   You can make _____ different models.

_____

4. Quinn, Roger, and Heather are playing a game. They each want a chance to be first. List the ways they will have to take turns to play first.

Math at Home Activity: Ask your child to list the order of children playing the game in Exercise 4

Name _____

Place Value to 1,000

Main Idea

I will use expanded form to write numbers up to 1,000.

Vocabulary

expanded form

Place value tells the value of a digit in a number.

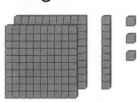

hundreds	tens	ones
2	1	3

Think
You can write a number in **expanded form**.

2 hundreds 1 ten 3 ones

200 + 10 + 3

213

Check

Write the number in expanded form.
Then write the number.

1. 1 hundred 4 tens 9 ones

   _____ + _____ + _____

   _____

2. 1 hundred 2 tens 5 ones

   _____ + _____ + _____

   _____

Write the number.

3. 300 + 70 + 6 = _____

4. 200 + 30 + 1 = _____

Circle the value of the red digit.

5. 931

   300   30   3

6. 277

   200   20   2

7. **Talk About It** How are 562 and 265 the same?
   How are they different?

Write the number in expanded form.
Then write the number.

8. 8 hundreds 7 tens 0 ones

_____ + _____ + _____

_____

9. 9 hundreds 9 tens 9 ones

_____ + _____ + _____

_____

Write the number.

10. 600 + 30 + 8 = _____

11. 700 + 60 + 8 = _____

12 500 + 20 + 4 = _____

13. 200 + 70 + 2 = _____

Circle the value of the red digit.

14. 965

900   90   9

15. 673

300   30   3

16. 468

600   60   6

17. 890

800   80   8

H.O.T. Problem

18. Make it Right
Julio wrote 365 in expanded
form like this: 300 + 50 + 6.
Tell why Julio is wrong.
Then make it right.

_____

_____ + _____ + _____

Math at Home Activity: Have your child tell you a three digit number.
Then ask your child to tell you the value of the first digit.

Name _____

Write each number in expanded form.

1. 420 = _____ + _____ + _____

2. 982 = _____ + _____ + _____

3. 570 = _____ + _____ + _____

4. 308 = _____ + _____ + _____

5. 255 = _____ + _____ + _____

Write the number. Color all of the butterflies that are greater than 500 yellow. Color all of the butterflies that are less than 500 purple.

6. 500 + 0 + 3 = _____

7. 300 + 20 + 5 = _____

8. 600 + 70 + 4 = _____

9. 400 + 0 + 6 = _____

10. 900 + 10 + 0 = _____

11. 800 + 0 + 1 = _____

Butterfly Fun

Place Value

What You Need

- paper and pencil

Play with a partner.

- Roll the three times.
- Roll 1 is the hundreds place, roll 2 is the tens place, roll 3 is the ones place.
- Write the number and say it out loud.
- Have your partner check your work.
- If correct, color a butterfly.
- The first person to color more butterflies wins!

Name _____

Read and Write Numbers to 1,000

Copyright © Macmillan/McGraw-Hill, a division of The McGraw-Hill Companies, Inc.

Get Ready

Main Idea

I will read and write numbers to 1,000.

Vocabulary

thousand

You can read and write numbers with symbols and words. Write 538.

1 one	11 eleven	10 ten	100 one hundred
2 two	12 twelve	20 twenty	200 two hundred
3 three	13 thirteen	30 thirty	300 three hundred
4 four	14 fourteen	40 forty	400 four hundred
5 five	15 fifteen	50 fifty	500 five hundred
6 six	16 sixteen	60 sixty	600 six hundred
7 seven	17 seventeen	70 seventy	700 seven hundred
8 eight	18 eighteen	80 eighty	800 eight hundred
9 nine	19 nineteen	90 ninety	900 nine hundred
			1,000 one **thousand**

Number name: five hundred thirty-eight

Check

Write the number in words.

1. 710

_____

2. 900

_____

Write the number.

3. thirty-eight

_____

4. one hundred twenty-one

_____

5.  Explain how you would write these numbers in words: 62 and 602.

Write the number in words.

6. 226

_____

7. 306

_____

8. 1,000

_____

9. 186

_____

10. 720

_____

11. 602

_____

Write the number.

12. one thousand

_____

13. seven hundred eighteen

_____

14. six hundred fourteen

_____

15. nine hundred one

_____

16. three hundred sixty

_____

17. six hundred fifty-one

_____

Problem Solving

18. **Critical Thinking** Chico shows 999 with base ten blocks. He adds I more ▪. What number is he showing now? _____.

How do you know?

_____

_____

326 three hundred twenty-six

Math at Home Activity: Say three hundred forty-seven and have your child write the number.

Name _____

Write how many hundreds, tens, and ones.

1.

_____ hundreds = _____ tens = _____ ones

Write how many hundreds, tens, and ones.
Then write the number.

2.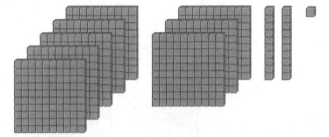

hundreds	tens	ones

_____

Write the number in expanded form. Then write the number.

3. five hundred sixty-six

_____ + _____ + _____

_____

4. nine hundred ten

_____ + _____ + _____

_____

5. 700 + 20 + 6 = _____

6. 300 + 70 + 7 = _____

Circle the value of the red digit.

7. 157

500   50   5

8. 963

900   90   9

9. 505

500   50   5

Write the number.

10. nine hundred ninety-eight

_____

11. five hundred one

_____

three hundred twenty-seven

Write how many ones. Then write how many tens.

12.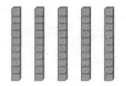

_____ ones = _____ tens

13.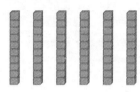

_____ ones = _____ tens

Estimate about how many? Circle your answer.

14.

about 20   about 40   about 60

15.

about 10   about 50   about 70

Use the tally chart to complete the pictograph.
Answer the questions.

Favorite School Subject		
Subject	Tally	Total
Reading	||	
Science	Ж|	
Math	||||	
Art	||	

Favorite School Subject	
Reading	
Science	
Math	
Art	

Key: 📖 = 2

16. How many students like art or reading? _____

17. How many students were surveyed in all? _____

18. How many students chose math as their favorite? _____

Formative Assessment

Name _____

Problem-Solving Investigation

Main Idea

I will choose a strategy to solve a problem.

Your Mission:
Find out how many yellow marbles Amy has.

I have marbles in 4 different colors. I have 106 blue marbles, 235 pink, 84 yellow, and 113 green marbles. My friend gave me 100 more yellow marbles. How many yellow marbles do I have now?

Understand

What do I know? Underline what you know.

What do I need to find out? Circle it.

Plan

How will I solve the problem?
One way is to use models and act it out.

Solve

Act it Out.

Amy has _____ yellow marbles.

Check

Look Back
Does my answer make sense?

Mixed Problem Solving

Choose a strategy. Solve.

1. Stevie has some pennies. He puts the pennies into 3 groups to count them. He has 80 pennies in the first group, 3 pennies in the second group, and 500 pennies in the third group. How many pennies does he have?

_____ pennies

2. Marta's family is going to visit her cousins. They will drive for 3 days. Each day they will drive 300 miles. How far is it to Marta's cousins' house?

_____ miles

3. The school cafeteria sells 50 bananas every day. How many bananas do they sell in 5 days?

_____ bananas

4. Jack had $1.00. Then he found two coins. Now he has $1.15. What two coins did he find?

_____ and _____

Math at Home Activity: Take advantage of problem-solving opportunities during daily routines such as riding in the car, bedtime, doing laundry, putting away groceries, planning schedules, and so on.

Name _____

Compare Numbers

Main Idea

I will compare numbers using symbols.

To compare larger numbers first compare the hundreds. If the hundreds are equal, compare the tens. If the tens are equal, compare the ones.

Greater than >	Less than <	Equal to =
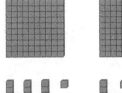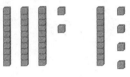	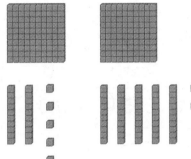	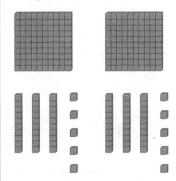
132 is greater than 114.	125 is less than 152.	135 is equal to 135.
132 > 114	125 < 152	135 = 135

✓ Check

Compare. Write >, <, or =.

1. 142 ◯> 124

2. 253 ◯ 257

3. 313 ◯ 313

4. 842 ◯ 795

5. 694 ◯ 694

6. 203 ◯ 153

7. 100 ◯ 1,000

8. 999 ◯ 99

9. 133 ◯ 133

10. **Talk About It** Explain how you compare 567 and 576.

Compare. Write >, <, or =.

11. 150 ◯ 150   **12.** 132 ◯ 213

13. 689 ◯ 627   **14.** 425 ◯ 425

15. 907 ◯ 899   **16.** 533 ◯ 533

17. 207 ◯ 210   **18.** 697 ◯ 667   **19.** 108 ◯ 801

20. 411 ◯ 421   **21.** 619 ◯ 621   **22.** 290 ◯ 280

23. 729 ◯ 729   **24.** 325 ◯ 300   **25.** 565 ◯ 569

26. 332 ◯ 335   **27.** 984 ◯ 894   **28.** 239 ◯ 239

Problem Solving

29. Logical Reasoning What number am I? I am greater than 3 hundreds, 2 tens, and 2 ones. I am less than 3 hundreds, 2 tens, 4 ones.

_____

Make up your own problem. Ask a friend to solve it.

_____

_____

_____

_____

Math at Home Activity: Ask your child to name numbers that are greater than, less than, and equal to 807.

Name _____

Order Numbers

Main Idea

I will use place value to put numbers in order.

Use place value to order these numbers from **least** to **greatest.**

316, 298, and 314

First, compare the hundreds.

316   **2**98   **3**14

> 200 is less than 300.

316 and 314 have the same hundreds. **Next,** compare the tens.

31̲6   31̲4

> 316 and 314 both have 1 ten.

Since the hundreds and tens are the same compare the ones.

314   316

> 314 is less than 316.

298, 314, 316

✓ Check

> **Remember**
> Compare the hundreds, tens and then ones to order the numbers.

Write the numbers from **least** to **greatest.**

1. 592, 600, 589

_____, _____, _____

2. 601, 585, 590

_____, _____, _____

Write the numbers from **greatest** to **least.**

3. 492, 325, 530

_____, _____, _____

4. 765, 762, 627

_____, _____, _____

5. How do you use place value to order numbers?

 **Practice**

> Remember
Look at the hundreds first, then the tens and the ones.

Write the numbers from **least** to **greatest**.

6. 798, 805, 801

_____ , _____ , _____ .

7. 800, 795, 799

_____ , _____ , _____

8. 802, 799, 813

_____ , _____ , _____

9. 795, 815, 807, 1,000

_____ , _____ , _____ , _____

10. 808, 812, 801, 821

_____ , _____ , _____ , _____

11. 172, 236, 242, 221

_____ , _____ , _____ , _____

Write the numbers from **greatest** to **least**.

12. 427, 522, 431

_____ , _____ , _____

13. 676, 629, 668

_____ , _____ , _____

14. 602, 599, 610

_____ , _____ , _____

15. 574, 598, 580

_____ , _____ , _____

16. 871, 718, 817, 781

_____ , _____ , _____ , _____

17. 400, 397, 411, 409

_____ , _____ , _____ , _____

H.O.T. Problem

18. Make It Right

Maria put numbers in order from greatest to least.
Tell why Maria is wrong.
Then make it right.

545 505 550

_____

_____

334 three hundred thirty-four

Math at Home Activity: Name 3 three-digit numbers and ask your child to write them down and put them in order from least to greatest.

Copyright © Macmillan/McGraw-Hill, a division of The McGraw-Hill Companies, Inc.

Name _____

Number Patterns

Main Idea

I will find number patterns.

Number patterns can help you count. In these patterns, each number is **more**.

548
547
546
545

575
565
555
545

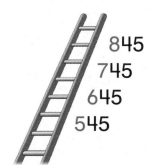
845
745
645
545

Count by ones.
Each number is
1 more.

Count by tens.
Each number is
10 more.

Count by
hundreds.
Each number is
100 more.

Check

Remember
Patterns can also be 100 less, 10 less, or 1 less.

Write the missing numbers.
Then write the counting pattern.

1. 340, 350, 360, _____ , 380

   The pattern is _____ .

2. 578, 579, _____ , 581, _____

   The pattern is _____ .

3. 941, 841, _____ , 641, 541

   The pattern is _____ .

4. 679, 678, _____ , _____ , 675

   The pattern is _____ .

5. **Talk About It** How can you tell if a number pattern is counting by hundreds?

Copyright © Macmillan/McGraw-Hill, a division of The McGraw-Hill Companies, Inc.

Write the missing numbers.
Then write the counting pattern.

6. 500, 510, _____, 530, _____

The pattern is _____.

7. 312, _____, 314, _____, 316

The pattern is _____.

8. 800, 790, 780, _____, 760

The pattern is _____.

9. 655, _____, 455, 355, _____

The pattern is _____.

10. _____, 486, 586, 686, _____

The pattern is _____.

11. 700, _____, 900

The pattern is _____.

12. 234, _____, _____, 264, 274

The pattern is _____.

13. _____, 519, 518, 517, _____

The pattern is _____.

Problem Solving

14. Critical Thinking Each week, the cafeteria orders 200 pizzas. The pizza is sold at lunch every Friday in January. If there are 4 Fridays in January, how many total pizzas does the cafeteria order in January?

_____ pizzas

Friday	Pizzas
1	200
2	400
3	600
4	?

Math at Home Activity: Pick a 3-digit number. Ask your child to count by ones, tens, or hundreds.

Florence Parpart invented the refrigerator more than 94 years ago. It was hard to keep food cold before that!

Look at the number 94. What number is in the ones place?

_____

Circle which item was invented first. Why do you think so?

School desk

Windshield wipers

Refrigerator

_____
_____
_____

FOLD DOWN

Problem Solving
in Social Sciences

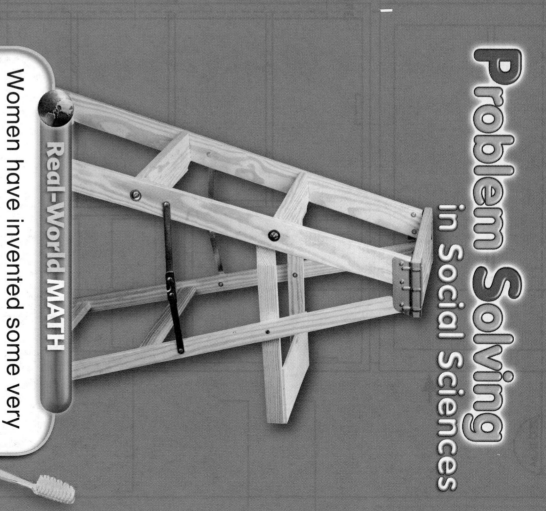

Real-World MATH

Women have invented some very useful things.

This book belongs to

_____

Copyright © Macmillan/McGraw-Hill, a division of The McGraw-Hill Companies, Inc.

A

Mary Anderson came up with the idea for windshield wipers over 105 years ago. Just think how hard it would be to drive if it were not for Mary!

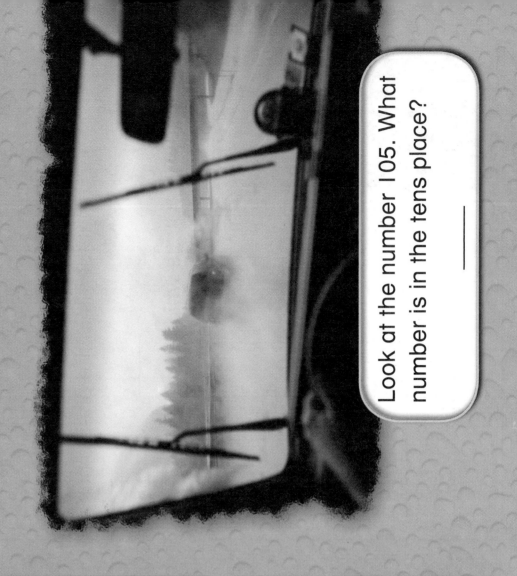

Look at the number 105. What number is in the tens place?

_____

Anna Breadin invented the school desk more than 119 years ago. Does it look like the desk you use now?

Look at the number 119. What number is in the hundreds place?

_____

Name _____

Vocabulary

Fill in the blank. Use the word bank.

1. I am the left digit of a three digit number.

   What am I? _____

2. You can use me to write a number in a different way.

   What am I? _____

Word Bank

expanded form
hundreds

Concepts

Write how many hundreds, tens, and ones.

3.

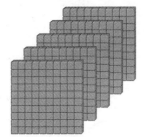

_____ hundreds = _____ tens = _____ ones

Write how many hundreds, tens, and ones.
Then write the number.

4.

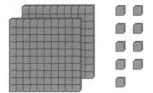

hundreds	tens	ones

_____

Write the number in expanded form.
Then write the number.

5. 5 hundred 6 tens 0 ones

   _____ + _____ + _____

   _____

6. 8 hundreds 7 tens 8 ones

   _____ + _____ + _____

   _____

Write the number.

7. $5 + 50 + 500$ _____

8. $200 + 90 + 7$ _____

Circle the value of the red digit.

9. 816

600 60 6

10. 159

100 10 1

11. 911

900 90 9

Write the number.

12. six hundred twenty-nine

_____

13. five hundred one

_____

Compare. Write >, <, or =.

14. 100 ◯ 1,000

15. 599 ◯ 600

16. 101 ◯ 101

Write the numbers from **greatest** to **least**.

17. 745, 457, 700

_____, _____, _____

18. 111, 100, 1000

_____, _____, _____

19. Natalie dropped these 4 cards:

660, 670, _____, 690

She is missing one.

Write the number. _____

20. David and Allison are counting like this: 500, 400, 300.

The pattern is _____.

Name _____

Listen as your teacher reads each problem.
Choose the correct answer.

A A number has six hundreds, four tens, and seven ones. What is the number?

776 746 647 467
○   ○   ○   ○

B What is another way to write eight hundred twenty-nine?

800 + 22 + 2   720 + 22
○   ○

800 + 20 + 9   700 + 20 + 4
○   ○

Listen as your teacher reads each problem.
Choose the correct answer.

1 What is the value of the three in three hundred ninety-one?

300 33 30 3
○   ○   ○   ○

4 What is another way to write five hundred eighty-three?

538 358 583 853
○   ○   ○   ○

2 What is another name for two hundred plus forty plus seven?

247 374 472 704
○   ○   ○   ○

5 Which number goes in the box?

427 < ☐

478 407 372 274
○   ○   ○   ○

3 Which number sentence is true?

632 < 623   632 > 623
○   ○

632 = 623   326 > 632
○   ○

6 Which of the following fractions is the greatest?

$\frac{1}{12}$ $\frac{1}{3}$ $\frac{1}{8}$ $\frac{1}{2}$
○   ○   ○   ○

7 Look at the fraction bars. Which fraction bar shows five-sixths shaded?

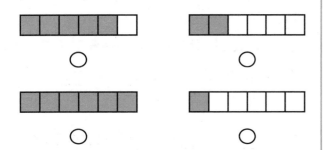

○   ○

○   ○

10 What is the solution to this problem?

$$\begin{array}{r} 80 \\ -\ 10 \\ \hline \end{array}$$

90   70   60   50

○   ○   ○   ○

8 Which drawing shows five times two?

5×2

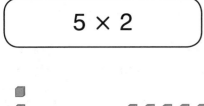

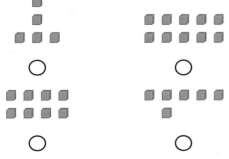

○   ○

○   ○

11 Which picture shows how three children should share nine apples equally?

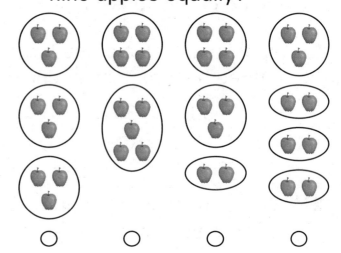

○   ○   ○   ○

9 Which number goes in the box?

$101 < \boxed{} < 103$

100   102   123   301

○   ○   ○   ○

12 What fractional part of this figure is shaded?

$\dfrac{1}{6}$ $\dfrac{1}{3}$ $\dfrac{1}{2}$ $\dfrac{1}{5}$

○   ○   ○   ○

Summative Assessment

STOP

Geometry

▷ **Key Vocabulary**

solid shapes
face
vertex
edge
plane shapes

Explore

There are many shapes in this picture. Name two that you see.

Name _____

Math Online

Take the Chapter Readiness
Quiz at ca.gr2math.com.

Are You Ready for Chapter 11?

Draw an X over the shape that is different.

1.

2.

Draw a line to match objects that are the
same shape.

3.

4.

5.

6. Li got a picture frame for her birthday.
What shape is it? Circle the word.

triangle   circle   rectangle

This page checks skills needed for Chapter 11.

Dear Family,
Today my class started Chapter 11, **Geometry**. In this chapter, I will learn about solid and plane shapes. Here is an activity we can do and a list of books we can read together.

Love,

_____

Activity

Have your child find at least two objects around your home that matches one of these shapes. Place the objects in a bag. Take turns closing your eyes, picking an object, and identifying the figure with your eyes closed.

sphere

pyramid

cube

rectangular prism

cylinder   cone

Key Vocabulary

face the flat part of a solid shape

vertex a point on a solid or plane shape where two or more edges meet

edge the line where two sides or faces meet

 Math Online Click on the eGlossary link at ca.gr2math.com to find out more about these words. There are 13 languages.

Books to Read

The Village of Round and Square Houses
by Ann Grifalconi
Little, Brown,
1986.

Captain Invincible and the Space Shapes
by Stuart J. Murphy
Harper Collins
Publishers, 2001.

The Greedy Triangle
by Marilyn Burns
Scholastic Press, 1995.

Estimada familia:

Hoy mi clase comenzó el Capítulo II, **La geometría**. En este capítulo, aprenderé sobre formas sólidas y planas. A continuación, hay una actividad que podemos hacer y una lista de libros que podemos leer juntos.

Cariños,

_____

Actividad

Pídanle a su hijo(a) que consiga alrededor de la casa por lo menos dos objetos que concuerden con una de estas formas. Coloquen los objetos en una bolsa. Con los ojos cerrados, túrnense para escoger un objeto e identificar la figura.

 esfera

 pirámide

cubo

prisma rectangular

 cilindro   cono

Vocabulario clave

cara la parte plana de una forma sólida

vértice un punto en una forma sólida o plana en donde se juntan dos o más caras

arista línea donde se juntan dos caras o lados

Math Online Visiten el enlace eGlossary en ca.gr2math.com para averiguar más sobre estas palabras, las cuales se muestran en 13 idiomas.

Libros recomendados

Figuras solidas
de Daniel Shepard
Red Brick, 2006.

Geometria:un vistazo a monstruopolis
de John Burstein
Gareth Stevens Publishing, 2006

Pulgada a pulgada
de Leo Lionni
Obolensky, 1960

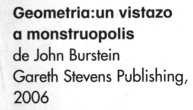

Name _____

Solid Shapes

Main Idea

I will identify solid shapes.

Vocabulary

solid shapes
sphere
cube
pyramid
cone
cylinder
rectangular prism

These are **solid shapes**. A solid shape is a 3-dimensional figure with length, width, and height.

 sphere

 cube

 pyramid

 cone

 cylinder

 rectangular prism

Check

Write the name of the shape. Circle the objects that are the same shape.

1.  _____

2. _____

3. _____

4. _____

5. **Talk About It** Name some objects that are the same shape as a cylinder.

Write the name of the shape.
Color the shapes that match.

6. _____

7. _____

8. _____

9. _____

10. _____

11. _____

Problem Solving

12. Visual Thinking Jose's
apartment building is shaped like
a rectangular prism. Draw what
the building might look like.

13. There are 38 windows on each
side of the building. If 2 window
washers each wash the same
number of windows, how many
will each wash?

_____ windows

Math at Home Activity: Find objects in the house that are the
same 3-dimensional shapes as those shown above. Ask your child to
name the shape.

Name _____

Faces, Edges, and Vertices

Get Ready

Main Idea

I will describe and classify solid shapes using faces, edges, and vertices.

Vocabulary

face

vertex (vertices)

edge

You can describe and classify solid shapes by the number of faces, edges, and vertices.

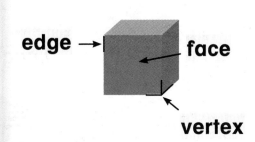

edge →   ← face

vertex

A **face** is a flat surface.

An **edge** is the line where 2 faces meet.

A **vertex** is the point where 3 or more faces meet.

✓ Check

Use solid shapes to count the faces, edges, and vertices.

	Shape	Faces	Edges	Vertices
1.	 cube	6	12	8
2.	rectangular prism	___	___	___
3.	pyramid	___	___	___
4.	cylinder	___	___	___
5.	cone	___	___	___
6.	sphere	___	___	___

7. **Talk About It** How are a rectangular prism and a cube alike?

Practice

Circle the objects that match the description.

Remember
Count the faces, edges, and vertices you cannot see.

8. 6 faces, 12 edges, 8 vertices

9. 0 faces, 0 edges, 0 vertices

10. 1 face, 0 edges, 1 vertex

11. 2 faces, 0 edges, 0 vertices

12. 5 faces, 8 edges, 5 vertices

13. 6 faces, 12 edges, 8 vertices

  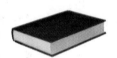

14. WRITING IN ▶MATH

Look at the two shapes. How are they alike?

_____

_____

How are they different?

_____

_____

Name each shape. _____ and _____

350 three hundred fifty

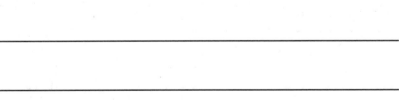

Math at Home Activity: Have your child identify and describe 3-dimensional figures that are in your home.

Name _____

Match the spiders to the correct shapes.
Be careful, some match to more than one shape!

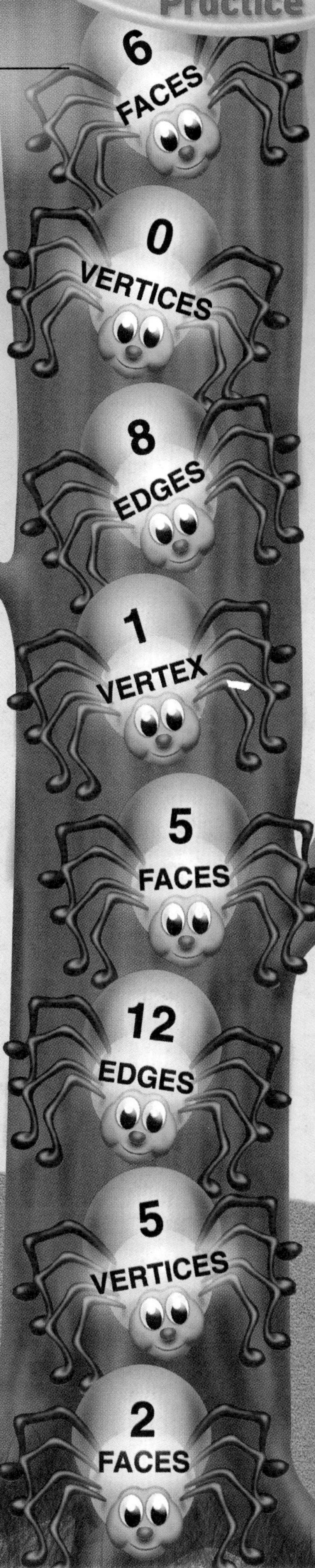

6 FACES

0 VERTICES

8 EDGES

1 VERTEX

5 FACES

12 EDGES

5 VERTICES

2 FACES

Game Time

Geometry Ball
Faces, Edges, and Vertices

You Will Need

Play with a partner:

- Roll the .
- Take turns. Move your ♟ that many spaces.
- Read the description. Name the shape.
- Use geometric solids to check answers.
- If you are incorrect, go back 1 space.
- Slide through the end zones.
- The first one to the Finish wins.

START	12 edges	0 edges	2 faces	0 faces	1 vertex	5 vertices	6 faces	8 edges	1 face	0 vertices	SLIDE
FINISH	10	20	30	40	50	40	30	20	10		↓↓↓↓↓
	10	20	30	40	50	40	30	20	10		
SLIDE	5 vertices	6 faces	0 vertices	8 edges	12 edges	8 vertices	0 edges	5 faces	1 vertex	0 faces	1 face

Name _____

Plane Shapes

Main Idea

I will identify plane shapes.

Vocabulary

plane shapes
parallelogram
hexagon
trapezoid

These are **plane shapes**. A plane shape is a 2-dimensional figure with only length and width.

circle   **triangle**   **square**   **rectangle**

parallelogram   **hexagon**   **trapezoid**

Check

Circle the shapes that match the name.

1. rectangle

2. triangle

3. trapezoid

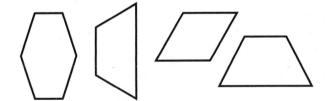

4. square

5. **Talk About It** How are squares and trapezoids alike? How are they different?

Color the shapes that match the name.

Name	Shape
6. parallelogram	
7. hexagon	
8. triangle	
9. circle	

H.O.T. Problem

10. Thinking Math Which shape does *not* belong? Circle it. Explain why it does not belong.

_____

_____

Math at Home Activity: Ask your child to draw a picture using as many of these shapes as possible.

Name _____

Problem-Solving Strategy
Find a Pattern

Main Idea

I will find a pattern to solve a problem.

Joanna is making a pattern that repeats 2 cubes and 3 spheres. She wants to use 30 shapes.
How many cubes will she need? How many spheres?

Understand

What do I know? Underline what you know.
What do I need to find? Circle the question.

Plan

How will I solve the problem?
I will find a pattern.

Solve

CCSSS   CCSSS   CCSSS

CCSSS   CCSSS   CCSSS

She will make _____ cubes and _____ spheres.

Check

Look Back
How can I check my answer?

Try It

Find a pattern to solve.

1. Sarah's flower garden has 10 rows of flowers. There are 4 flowers in the first row, 8 in the second, and 12 in the third. How many flowers are in the last row?

_____ flowers

2. A horse has two ears.
   Two horses have four ears.
   Three horses have six ears.
   How many ears do five horses have?

_____ ears

Your Turn

Find a pattern to solve.

3. One frog has four legs.
   Two frogs have eight legs.
   How many legs do three frogs have?

_____ legs

4. Kareem makes a pattern that repeats 1 hexagon and 5 trapezoids. What is the 13th shape in the pattern?

_____

5. For five days in a row, Jesse earned $9 and Kyle earned $3. How much money had the two earned after the fifth day?

_____

Math at Home Activity: Ask your child to tell you what pattern he or she used to solve Exercise 3.

Name _____

Write the name of the shape. Circle the
objects that match the shape.

1. _____

2. _____

Circle the objects that match the description.

3. 1 face, 0 edges, 1 vertex

4. 6 faces, 12 edges, 8 vertices

Color the shapes that match the name.

5. triangle

6. rectangle

7. hexagon

8. parallelogram

9. Jill and Alex each have a shape.
Both shapes have 6 faces, 12 edges,
and 8 vertices. Their shapes are not
the same. Name the two shapes.

_____ and _____

Skip count to find the value.

10.

_____ _____ _____ _____ _____ _____ _____ _____   _____ total

---

Find the value of these coins.

11.

_____ _____ _____ _____ _____ _____   _____ total

Add. Then multiply.

12.

_____ + _____ = _____

_____ × _____ = _____

Divide.

13. 8 ducks swim in 2 groups.

$8 \div 2 =$ _____

Each group has _____ ducks.

14. 12 toys are shared by 4 friends.

$12 \div 4 =$ _____

Each friend gets _____ toys.

---

15. Your teacher asks you to count the students in your class by 5s. There are 20 students in your class. Show how you would count.

_____

Formative Assessment

Name _____

Sides and Vertices

Get Ready

Main Idea

I will describe and classify plane shapes.

Vocabulary

side

Review Vocabulary

vertex (vertices)

You can describe and classify plane shapes by the number of sides and vertices.

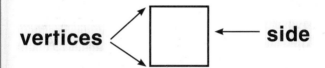

side → ← **vertices**

3 sides and 3 vertices

vertices ← ☐ ← **side**

4 sides and 4 vertices

○

0 sides and 0 vertices

A square has the same number of sides and vertices.

✓ Check

Write how many sides and vertices.

1. 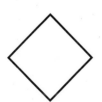   ___**4**___ sides

___**4**___ vertices

2. ▽   _____ sides

_____ vertices

3. ⬡   _____ sides

_____ vertices

4. ○   _____ sides

_____ vertices

5. **Talk About It** How are a square and a hexagon alike? How are they different?

Circle the shapes that match the description.

> **Remember**
> Plane shapes have the same number of sides and vertices.

6. 4 sides and
   4 vertices

7. 3 sides and
   3 vertices

8. 0 sides and
   0 vertices

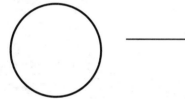

Write the name of the shape. Tell two things about it.

9. 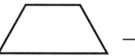 _____   _____

                                      _____

10. _____ _____   _____

                                      _____

Problem Solving

11. **Logical Reasoning** Are all squares rectangles?
    Are all rectangles squares? Explain.

    _____

    _____

Math at Home Activity: While driving, look at road signs together.
Ask your child to name and describe the shapes he or she sees.

Relate Plane Shapes to Solid Shapes

Main Idea

I will relate plane shapes to solid shapes.

Some solid shapes have faces that are plane shapes.

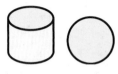

The face of the cylinder is a

_____.

Check

Use solid shapes. Trace around the face.
Circle the shape that you made. Name the shape.

1.
   △ □ ○   _____

2.
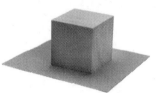   □ △ ▭   _____

3.
   □ ▭ △   _____

4. **Talk About It** Compare a sphere and a circle. How are they alike? How are they different?

Look at the picture. Draw the plane shape you would make if you traced one of the faces.

5.

6.

7.

8.

H.O.T. Problems

Explaining Math

9. Draw a picture of a shape that has no vertices and a curved edge.

10. Draw a picture of a shape that has 6 sides and 4 vertices. Is there such a shape?

Math at Home Activity: Have your child trace the faces of a box and a can. Ask them to name the plane shapes they traced.

Name _____

Make New Shapes

Get Ready

Main Idea

I will put shapes together to make new shapes. I will take shapes apart to make new shapes.

You can put shapes together and take them apart to make new shapes.

Put together 2 squares to make a rectangle.

 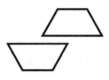

Take apart a hexagon to make 2 trapezoids.

Check

Use pattern blocks to make a new shape. Trace the shapes you used. Name the new shape.

1.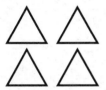

_____

2.

_____

3.

_____

4.

_____

5. **Talk About It** Describe how you would put these triangles together to make another shape.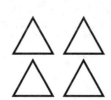

Trace each shape on another piece of paper.
Cut along the dashed line. Circle the new shapes
you made.

6.   rectangle   square   triangle   trapezoid

7.   triangle   parallelogram   rectangle   trapezoid

8.   parallelogram   triangle   square   hexagon

9.   hexagon   triangle   parallelogram   circle

Data File

In 1985, California named an official
state gemstone. It is a blue crystal that
is sometimes called a "blue diamond."
A diamond is a parallelogram. This blue
crystal is found inside California's state
rock, the serpentine.

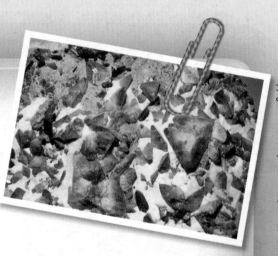

10. Use 2 triangles to make
a parallelogram or diamond.
Trace the shape you made.

Math at Home Activity: Ask your child to show you how to put
two squares together to make a new shape.

Problem-Solving Investigation

Main Idea

I will choose a strategy to solve the problem.

Your Mission:
Find the shape that is described.

I have a plane shape. It has 4 sides. All four sides have the same length. What is my shape?

Understand

What do I know? Underline what you know.
What do I need to find out? Circle it.

Plan

How will I solve the problem?
One way is to guess and check.

Solve

Guess and Check
Make a guess for an answer. Then check your answer to see if it is correct.

rectangle?

It has 4 sides, but the sides are not all equal.

square?

It has 4 sides, and they are all equal.

It could be a _____.

Check

Look Back
Does my answer make sense?
How can I check my answer?

Mixed Problem Solving

Choose a strategy. Solve.

Problem-Solving Strategies

- Guess and check
- Draw a picture
- Act it out

1. I have one face.
I also have no edges.
I do have one vertex.
What shape am I?

I am a _____.

2. Two different numbers have a sum of 9 and a product of 18. What are the numbers?

_____ and _____

3. Beth says she knows 2 different ways to make a hexagon with pattern block shapes. What blocks can she use?

_____ or _____

4. You have 5 coins that total $0.75. What coins do you have?

_____

5. Lilla had 39 baseball cards. She traded some with her friend Lou. She gave him 12 cards and got 9 cards from Lou. How many cards did Lilla have then?

_____ cards

 Math at Home Activity: Take advantage of problem-solving opportunities during daily routines such as riding in the car, bedtime, doing laundry, putting away groceries, planning schedules, and so on.

Copyright © Macmillan/McGraw-Hill, a division of The McGraw-Hill Companies, Inc.

What shape do you see?

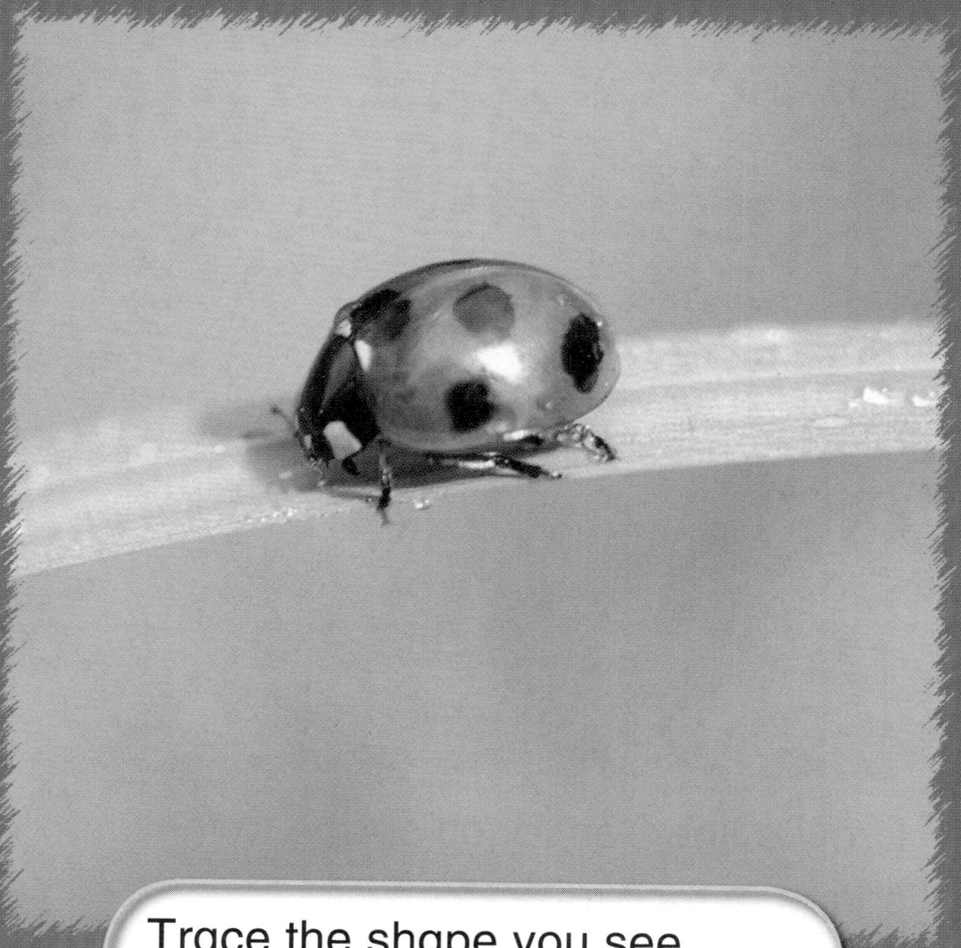

Trace the shape you see.
Use a piece of paper.
Create your own picture using all the shapes you know.

FOLD DOWN

Problem Solving in Science

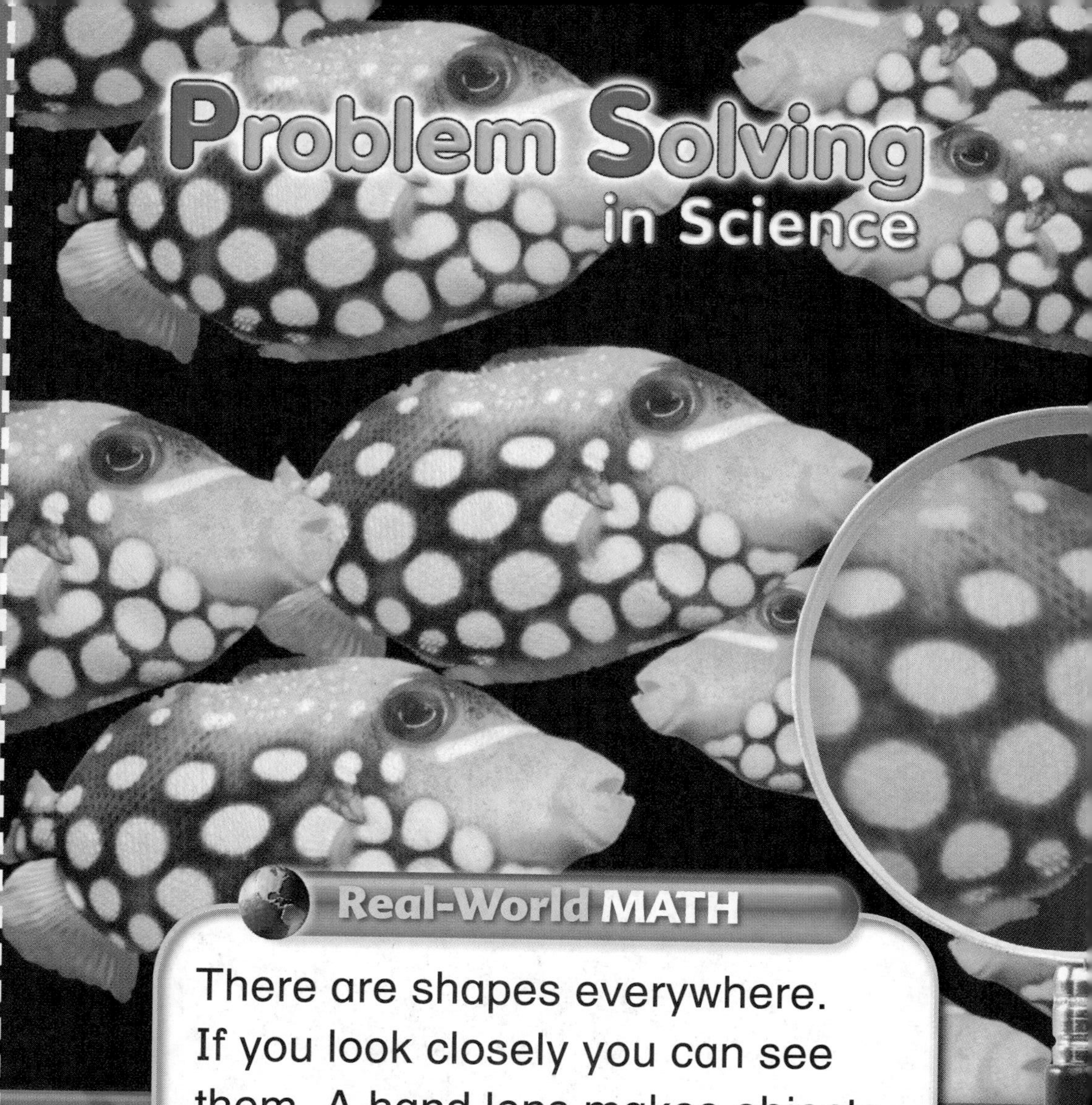

Real-World MATH

There are shapes everywhere. If you look closely you can see them. A hand lens makes objects look larger.

This book belongs to

____

There are many shapes here.
Can you find them all?

Draw a line from each shape to the shape in the web.

What shape do you see?

_____

C

B

Name _____

Vocabulary

Fill in the blanks.

1. A circle is a _____.

2. A triangle has 3 _____.

3. _____ have length, width and height.

4. A _____ is where edges or sides meet.

Concepts

Write the name of the shape.
Color the shapes that match

5. _____

6. _____

Circle the objects that match the description.

7. 2 faces, 0 edges, 0 vertices

8. 6 faces, 12 edges, 8 vertices

Color the shapes that match the name.

Name	Shape
9. hexagon	
10. parallelogram	

Circle the shape that matches the description.

11. 0 sides and 0 vertices

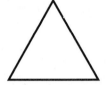 

Write how many sides and vertices.

12.  _____ sides

_____ vertices

13. 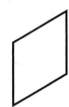 _____ sides

_____ vertices

Look at the picture. Draw the plane shape you would make if you traced one of the faces.

14.

15.

16. Dani bought a toy at the toy store. Her toy has 0 faces, 0 edges, and 0 vertices.

What did Dani buy at the store? _____

Explain your answer.

_____

_____

17. Randy's favorite plane shape has 4 sides and 4 vertices. List three shapes that could be Randy's favorite.

_____, _____ or _____

Summative Assessment

Name _____

Listen as your teacher reads each problem.
Choose the correct answer.

A Look at the sphere and then at the objects. Which object has the same shape as the sphere?

○   ○   ○   ○

B How many faces does a rectangular prism have?

0	4	5	6
○	○	○	○

Listen as your teacher reads each problem.
Choose the correct answer.

1 Look at the two triangles. Which of the following shapes can be made from the two triangles?

○   ○   ○   ○

3 Which number goes in the box?

532 > ☐

678	557	612	469
○	○	○	○

2 Look at the pair of shapes. Which is a pair of triangles?

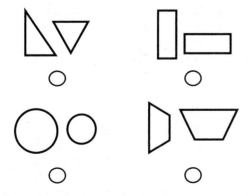

○   ○

○   ○

4 Look at the pyramid. How many vertices does the pyramid have?

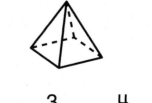

I	3	4	5
○	○	○	○

Chapter 11

5 Look at the numbers. Which number has 3 tens and 4 ones?

234   341   437   483
 ○   ○   ○   ○

6 Look at the fraction circles. Which fraction circle shows $\frac{1}{4}$ shaded?

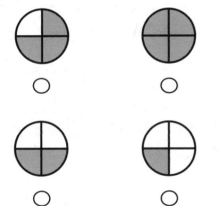

 ○   ○

 ○   ○

7 Which of the following fractions is the least?

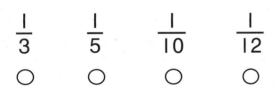

$\frac{1}{3}$ $\frac{1}{5}$ $\frac{1}{10}$ $\frac{1}{12}$
 ○   ○   ○   ○

8 What is another way to write twenty-nine cents?

$2.90 $0.29
 ○   ○

$29 $2.09
 ○   ○

9 Keegan did this subtraction problem. Which addition problem shows that she got the right answer?

$$\begin{array}{r} 45 \\ -\ 24 \\ \hline 21 \end{array}$$

$$\begin{array}{r} 21 \\ +\ 24 \\ \hline \end{array} \quad \begin{array}{r} 45 \\ +\ 24 \\ \hline \end{array} \quad \begin{array}{r} 24 \\ -\ 69 \\ \hline \end{array} \quad \begin{array}{r} 69 \\ -\ 69 \\ \hline \end{array}$$

 ○   ○   ○   ○

10 Shane has two trapezoids. Which of the following shapes can be made from the two trapezoids?

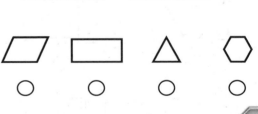

 ○   ○   ○   ○

CHAPTER 12

Measurement and Time

Key Vocabulary

measure
length
inch
centimeter
quarter hour

Explore

About how tall do you think she is? Circle it.

2   or   4

Are You Ready for Chapter 12?

Write the length.

1.

_____ cubes

2.

_____ cubes

Circle the time.

3.

5 o'clock
4 o'clock
3 o'clock

4.

7 o'clock
2 o'clock
6 o'clock

5.

10:30
10:00
2:30

6.

5:30
5:00
5:15

7. Bo brushes his teeth at 7:00 every morning.
This morning, he was a half hour late.
On the clock below, draw the time Bo
brushed his teeth today.

This page checks skills needed for Chapter 12.

Dear Family,

Today my class started Chapter 12, **Measurement and Time**. In this chapter, I will learn to use customary and metric units of measurement. I will also learn about time and how to measure it. Here is an activity we can do and a list of books we can read together.

Love,

_____

Activity

Have your child use a ruler to measure the length of a table in inches and centimeters. Which unit of measurement is the number greater?

Key Vocabulary

measure to find length, height, weight, capacity, or temperature using nonstandard and standard units

length how long or far something is

quarter hour one-fourth of an hour or 15 minutes of an hour

Math Online Click on the eGlossary link at ca.gr2math.com to find out more about these words. There are 13 languages.

Books to Read

Clocks and More Clocks
by Pat Hutchins
Aladdin, 1994.

How Tall, How Short, How Far Away
by David A. Adler
Holiday House, Inc.,
2000.

Inch by Inch
by Leo Lionni
HarperCollins
Publishers, 1995.

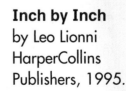

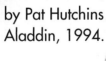

MATEMÁTICAS en CASA

Estimada familia:

Hoy mi clase comenzó el Capítulo 12, **La medición y la hora**. En este capítulo, aprenderé a usar unidades de medidas inglesas y métricas. También aprenderé acerca de la hora y cómo medirla. A continuación, hay una actividad que podemos hacer y una lista de libros que podemos leer juntos.

Cariños,

_____

Actividad

Pídanle a su hijo(a) que use una regla para medir la longitud de una mesa en centímetros y en pulgadas. ¿Con qué unidad de medida es mayor el número de la medida?

Vocabulario clave

medir calcular el largo, la altura, la capacidad o la temperatura usando unidades estándares y no estándares

longitud el largo de alguna cosa o la distandia hasta algo

cuarto de hora un cuarto de hora ó 15 minutos de una hora

Math Online Visiten el enlace eGlossary en ca.gr2math.com para averiguar más sobre estas palabras, las cuales se muestran en 13 idiomas.

Libros recomendados

La limonada de lulú
de Alma Ramirez
The Kane Press, 2006.

Vamos a medir
de Neil Ardley
Alianza, 1998.

¡Ya era hora, max!
de Kitty Richards
The Kane Press, 2006.

Name _____

Nonstandard Units

Get Ready

> I will estimate first. I think the pencil is about 6 cubes long.

Main Idea

I will estimate length.

Vocabulary

measure

length

Length is how long an object is. You can estimate the length of an object.

Estimate. The pencil is

about ___6___ cubes long.

Measure to see how close your estimate is.

Remember
Line up the end of the pencil with the end of the cube.

The pencil measures

about ___6___ cubes long.

Check

Find the object. Estimate. Then use 🎲 to measure.

1.

Estimate: about _____ 🎲

Measure: about _____ 🎲

2. 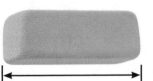 Glue Stick

Estimate: about _____ 🎲

Measure: about _____ 🎲

3. **Talk About It** What would your measure for Exercise 2 look like if you used paper clips?

Find the object. Estimate. Then use ⬡ to measure.

4.

Estimate: about _____ ⬡

Measure: about _____ ⬡

5.

Estimate: about _____ ⬡

Measure: about _____ ⬡

6.

Estimate: about _____ ⬡

Measure: about _____ ⬡

Problem Solving

7. Critical Thinking Estimate the length of your shoe in new crayons.

_____ crayons long

Estimate the length of your shoe in new pencils.

_____ pencils long

Now measure the length of your shoe. Use a new crayon and a new pencil.

_____ crayons long

_____ pencils long

Are your answers the same or different?

Explain why. _____

_____

_____

Math at Home Activity: Ask your child to estimate and then measure the length of a spoon using pennies, make sure the pennies touch.

Hands-On Activity

Measure to the Nearest Inch

Get Ready

Main Idea

I will use an inch ruler to measure.

Vocabulary

inch

Use an **inch** ruler to measure length.

First, line up the object with the end of the ruler starting at zero.

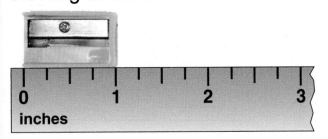

Next, look at the marks on the ruler. Find the measurement that is closest to the end of the object.

This pencil sharpener is about

_____ inch long.

Check

Find the object. Estimate. Then use an inch ruler to measure.

Find	Estimate	Measure
1. 	about _____ inches	about _____ inches
2.	about _____ inches	about _____ inches

3. **Talk About It** Describe how you use an inch ruler to measure.

 **Practice**

Find the object. Estimate. Measure to the
nearest inch.

Find	Estimate	Measure
4. Dictionary	about _____ inches	about _____ inches
5.	about _____ inches	about _____ inches
6.	about _____ inches	about _____ inches
7. Chalkboard Eraser	about _____ inches	about _____ inches
8.	about _____ inches	about _____ inches

Problem Solving

9. **Thinking Math** A large paper clip is about
2 inches long. How long is a chain of 4 paper
clips?

about _____ inches

 Math at Home Activity: Ask your child to show you how to measure
the length of a piece of yarn or string with an inch ruler.

Name _____

Inch, Foot, and Yard

Get Ready

Main Idea

I will measure objects in inches, feet, and yards.

Vocabulary

foot

yard

Use a yardstick to measure longer objects.

The door is about 1 yard long.

1 **foot** = 12 inches   1 **yard** = 3 feet or 36 inches

Check

Find the object. Use inches, feet, or yards. Estimate.
Measure each object in the unit shown.

Find	Estimate	Measure
1.	about _____ inches	about _____ inches
2.	about _____ feet	about _____ feet

3. **Talk About It** Would you use inches or feet to measure the length of your classroom? Explain.

Find the object. Use inches, feet, or yards. Estimate.
Measure each object.

Find	Estimate	Measure
4.	about _____ feet	about _____ feet
5.	about _____ yards	about _____ yards
6.	about _____ inches	about _____ inches
7.	about _____ yards	about _____ yards
8.	about _____ inches	about _____ inches

9. **WRITING IN ►MATH** Record two items that
could be measured in:

inches _____

feet _____

yards _____

Explain your thinking. _____

_____

Math at Home Activity: Ask your child to identify some objects
in your home that are 1 inch, 1 foot, and 1 yard long.

Problem-Solving Strategy
Use Logical Reasoning

Main Idea

I will use logical reasoning to solve problems.

Koko wants to plant a garden. She cannot decide if it should be 10 inches, 10 feet, or 100 yards long.

About how long should the garden be?

Understand

What do I know? Underline what you know.

What do I need to find out? Circle the question.

Plan

How will I solve the problem?

I will use logical reasoning.

Solve

I know 10 inches is too small.

10 feet makes the most sense.

100 yards does not make sense. It's too large.

Check

Look Back

Does my answer make sense?

What helped me decide to choose 10 feet?

Try It

Use logical reasoning to solve.

1. Sam planted a tomato plant that is
   1 foot tall. The bush grows a little each
   week. After 4 weeks, would the plant be
   10 inches or 14 inches tall?

   _____

2. Jane made a paper chain 1 yard long.
   Brad made a paper chain 2 feet long.
   Who made the longer paper chain?

   _____

Your Turn

Use logical reasoning to solve.

3. Mr. Moore's class is visiting the park. They are
   collecting things to measure. Lisa finds a
   pinecone. Would the pinecone be 3 inches,
   3 feet, or 3 yards long?

   _____

4. Dave is more than 40 inches tall.
   He is less than 43 inches tall.
   He is not 41 inches tall.
   How tall is Dave?

   _____

Math at Home Activity: Ask your child to estimate distances
from one room to another. Have your child check by measuring.

Name _____

Measure to the nearest inch.

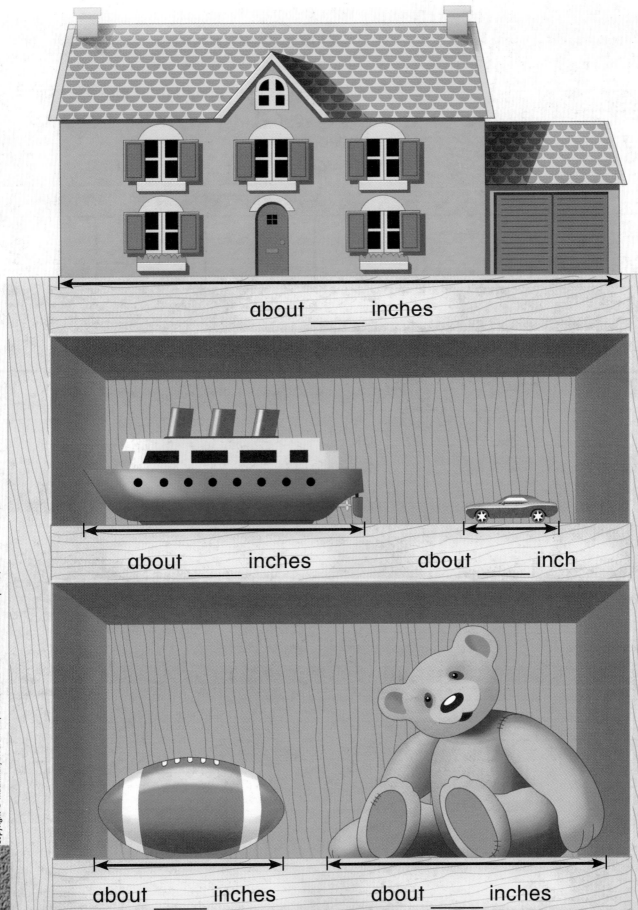

about ____ inches

about ____ inches   about ____ inch

about ____ inches   about ____ inches

Inching Along
Measurement

Play with a partner.
- Roll the .
- Find the number in the chart.
- Choose the best unit to measure the object.
- Move your ♟ the number of spaces you rolled.
- The first person to Finish wins!

You Will Need

-
- ♟

0	1	2	3	4	5

Start

Inch = 1 space
Feet = 2 spaces
Yard = 3 spaces

Finish

Name _____

Hands-On Activity

Measure to the Nearest Centimeter

Main Idea

I will use a centimeter ruler to measure.

Vocabulary

centimeter

Use a **centimeter** ruler to measure shorter objects.

First, line up the object with the end of the centimeter ruler starting at zero.

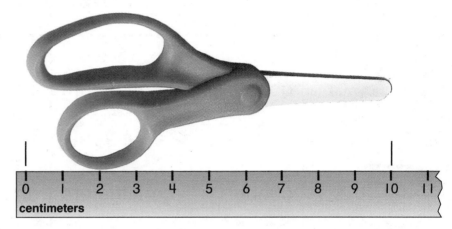

Next, look at the marks on the ruler. Find the measurement that is closest to the end of the object.

The scissors are about __10__ centimeters long.

Check

Find the object. Estimate. Then use a centimeter ruler to measure.

Find	Estimate	Measure
1. 	about ____ centimeters	about ____ centimeters
2.	about ____ centimeters	about ____ centimeters

3. **Talk About It** Would you use centimeters to measure the playground? Explain.

Practice

Find the object. Estimate. Then use a centimeter ruler to measure.

Find	Estimate	Measure
4.	about _____ centimeters	about _____ centimeters
5.	about _____ centimeters	about _____ centimeters
6. Glue Stick	about _____ centimeters	about _____ centimeters
7.	about _____ centimeters	about _____ centimeters
8.	about _____ centimeters	about _____ centimeters

Problem Solving

9. Thinking Math About how many centimeters long is this dollar bill? Write your answer.

_____ centimeters

Math at Home Activity: Ask your child to measure a newspaper or cabinet using a centimeter ruler.

388 three hundred eighty-eight

Centimeter and Meter

Get Ready

Main Idea

I will measure in centimeters and meters.

Vocabulary

meter

Use a meterstick to measure longer objects.

This doorway is about 1 **meter** wide.

1 **meter** = 100 centimeters

Check

Find the object. Estimate. Measure each object in the unit shown.

Find	Estimate	Measure
1. 	about _____ centimeters	about _____ centimeters
2.	about _____ meters	about _____ meters

3. **Talk About It** Would you use a centimeter ruler or a meterstick to measure the hallway? Explain.

Find the object. Estimate.
Measure each object in the unit shown.

Find	Estimate	Measure
4.	about ____ centimeters	about ____ centimeters
5.	about ____ meters	about ____ meters
6.	about ____ centimeters	about ____ centimeters
7.	about ____ meters	about ____ meters

H.O.T. Problem

8. Measure the bird's footprint. Use an inch ruler
and a centimeter ruler. Are there a greater
number of centimeters than inches?
Why?

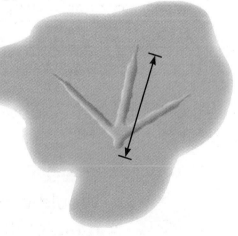

_____

_____

_____

Math at Home Activity: Have your child identify objects he or she
would measure using a centimeter ruler and objects he or she would
measure using a meterstick.

Name _____

Estimate. Then use 🎲 to measure.

1. 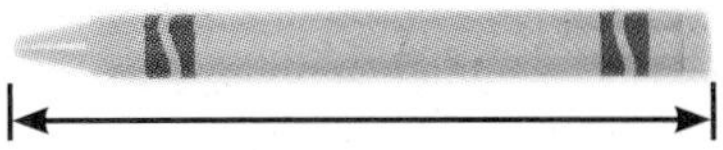 Estimate: about _____ 🎲

Measure: about _____ 🎲

Find the object. Use inches, feet, or yards. Estimate.
Measure each object.

Find	Estimate	Measure
2. 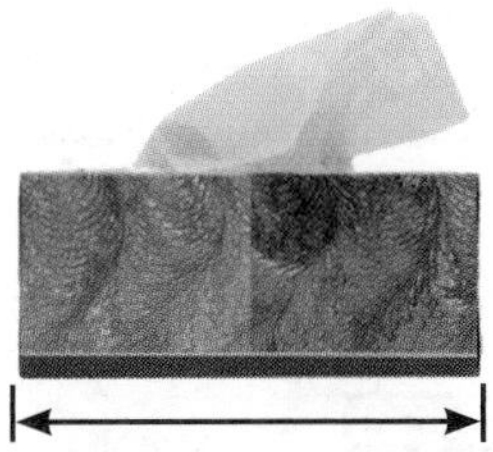	about _____ inches	about _____ inches
3. 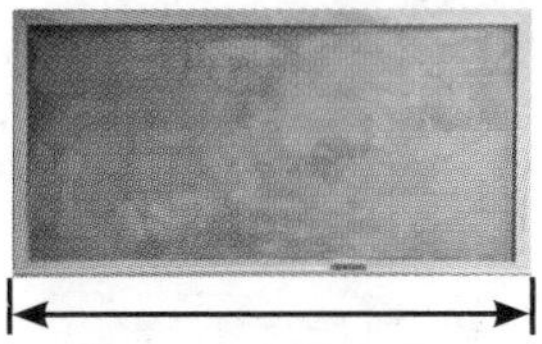	about _____ feet	about _____ feet
4. 	about _____ yards	about _____ yards

Find the objects. Use centimeters or meters. Estimate.
Measure each object.

Find	Estimate	Measure
5. 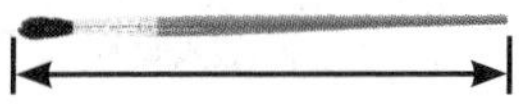	about _____ centimeters	about _____ centimeters
6. 	about _____ meters	about _____ meters

Spiral Review   Chapters 1–12

Write the fraction.

7.

number of colored parts ☐
―――――――――――
total number of parts ☐

8.

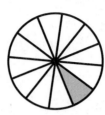

number of colored parts ☐
―――――――――――
total number of parts ☐

Write the fraction. Circle the fraction that equals 1.

9.

____

10.

____

11.

____

Add or subtract.

12.   27
        + 3
        ―――

13.   52
        − 33
        ―――

14.   81
         − 6
        ―――

15.   44
        + 44
        ―――

16. Erica wants to share her books with 4 of
her friends. She has 12 books she can share.
How many books will each one get? _____ books

> **Remember**
> Do not forget
> Erica.

Are there any books left over? _____

If so, how many are left? _____

392   three hundred ninety-two

Formative Assessment

Name _____

Time to the Quarter Hour

Get Ready

Main Idea

I will use a clock to tell time to the quarter hour.

Vocabulary

quarter hour

There are 15 minutes in a **quarter hour**.
Use a clock to measure time to the quarter hour.

quarter past 1   half past 1   quarter till 2

1:00   1:15   1:30   1:45

Check

Use your . Draw the minute hand to show the time.

1.	2.	3.

1.

11:15

2.

8:30

3.

10:45

4.

6:45

5.

4:15

6.

9:30

7. **Talk About It** At 4:15, where is the minute hand?
Explain.

Use your . Draw the minute hand to show the time.

8.

7:45

9.

12:30

10.

2:15

11.

1:45

12.

3:30

13.

6:00

14.

12:45

15.

5:00

16.

4:15

H.O.T. Problem

17. Why is each 15-minute period called a quarter
of an hour?

_____

_____

_____

Math at Home Activity: Ask your child to tell you
the time on a clock at 6:15, 7:30, and 8:45.

Name _____

Problem-Solving Investigation

Main Idea

I will choose a strategy to solve problems.

Your Mission:
Find how many feet tall Holly is.

My teacher told the class to measure each other. I measured Holly with my eraser. 5 erasers are about I foot in length. Holly is 20 erasers tall. How many feet tall is she?

Understand

What do I know? Underline what you know.
What do I need to find out? Circle the question.

Plan

How will I solve the problem?
One way is to make a table.

Solve

Make a table.

erasers	5	10	15	20
feet	1	2	3	4

Holly is about _____ feet tall.

Check

Look back.
Did I answer the question?

Problem-Solving Strategies

- Make a table
- Draw a picture
- Logical reasoning

Choose a strategy. Solve.

1. There are 3 feet in a yard. The basketball court at school is 10 yards wide. How many feet wide is the court?

_____ feet

2. Jeff has to replace the tires on some bikes. He has 3 different types of bikes. There are 2 bikes of each type. How many tires does he need to replace?

_____

3. Robin's mom told her that the party started at 2:00. She said to leave at a quarter to 2:00. What time would Robin have to leave for the party?

_____

4. Marty is setting up his race cars. The black car is between the yellow car and the orange car. The orange car is between the red car and the black car. The yellow car is in front of the black car. Which car is last?

_____ car

Math at Home Activity: Take advantage of problem-solving opportunities during daily routines such as riding in the car, bedtime, doing laundry, putting away groceries, planning schedules, and so on.

Name _____

Elapsed Time

Get Ready

Main Idea

I will find elapsed time.

A second grade class took a field trip to the zoo. They got to the zoo at 9:00 and left at 1:00. How long was the class at the zoo?

Count on each hour.
The class was at the zoo for ___4___ hours.

Remember
11:00 to 12:00 is 1 hour. 12:00 to 1:00 is another hour.

Check

Use your . Write the times. Then write how much time has passed.

Activity	Start Time	End Time	Time Passed
1. We played football.	3 : 00	5 : 00	We played football for _____ hours.
2. We visited a farm.	___ : ___	___ : ___	We visited the farm for _____ hours.

Use your 🕐. Write the times.
Then write how much time has passed.

Activity	Start Time	End Time	Time Passed
3. We went on a picnic.	____:____	____:____	We were at the picnic for _____ hour.
4. We built a sandcastle.	____:____	____:____	We built a sandcastle for _____ hours.
5. We went swimming.	____:____	____:____	We were swimming for _____ hours.
6. We walked the dog.	____:____	____:____	It took _____ hour to walk the dog.

7. **Talk About It** If school starts at 9:00 and ends at 3:00, how many hours have passed?

GO on

Name _____

Activity	Start Time	End Time	Time Passed
8. We collected shells.	: ___ ___	: ___ ___	We collected shells for ____ hour.
9. We skated.	: ___ ___	: ___ ___	We skated for ____ hours.
10. We played baseball.	: ___ ___	: ___ ___	The baseball game was ____ hours.
11. We were in school.	: ___ ___	: ___ ___	We were in school for ____ hours.
12. We painted.	: ___ ___	: ___ ___	We painted for ____ hour.

Copyright © Macmillan/McGraw-Hill, a division of The McGraw-Hill Companies, Inc.

Use your 🕐. Write the times.
Then write how much time has passed.

Activity	Start Time	End Time	Time Passed
13. We rode bikes.	____ : ____	____ : ____	We rode bikes for _____ hours.
14. We played soccer.	____ : ____	____ : ____	We played soccer for _____ hours.

Data File

Angel Arellano found out that the Fresno Chaffee Zoo needed money for repairs. She wrote a letter asking everyone in Fresno to give $1 to the zoo. People all over Fresno started sending money to the zoo! Now the Fresno Chaffee Zoo has enough money for repairs, thanks to Angel.

15. The zoo opens at 8:00. It closes at 6:00 at night. How many hours is the zoo open?

_____ hours

Math at Home Activity: Look at the clock when you sit down to eat dinner. Look at the clock at bedtime. Discuss how much time has passed between dinner and bedtime.

Name _____

Time Relationships

Main Idea

I will select the best unit to measure time.

Choose the best units to measure time.

Time Relationships	
I minute	= 60 seconds
I hour	= 60 minutes
I day	= 24 hours
I week	= 7 days
I month	= about 4 weeks
I year	= 12 months or 52 weeks

✓ Check

Circle the best unit to measure the time for each event.

1. to sneeze

    seconds   hours

2. to get ready for school

    seconds   minutes

3. to walk the dog

    minutes   days

4. to build a house

    seconds   year

5. **Talk About It** How many seconds are in 2 minutes?

Circle the best unit to measure the time for each event.

6. to do the dishes

hours   minutes

7. to complete second grade

months   days

8. to go to the store

weeks   hours

9. to build a playground

day   month

10. to eat lunch

hours   minutes

11. to sharpen your pencil

seconds   hours

12. Mary went to the beach with her family for 4 weeks. How many days was Mary at the beach?

_____ days

Problem Solving

13. Critical Thinking How old are you to the nearest years, months, and days?

_____

How old will you be in 12 months?

_____

Explain. _____

Math at Home Activity: Look at a calendar together. Have your child pick a month. Ask him or her what date is the third Sunday of that month.

Someday you might be as tall as your parents!

Mary's dad is 6 feet tall. Mary thinks she will be as tall as her dad someday. Mary is 3 feet tall now. How much more does Mary have to grow?

_____

FOLD DOWN

D

Problem Solving
in Science

Real-World MATH

Everyone grows! How tall are you?

_____

This book belongs to

_____

A

Your feet grow too. You know you are growing when your shoes get too tight.

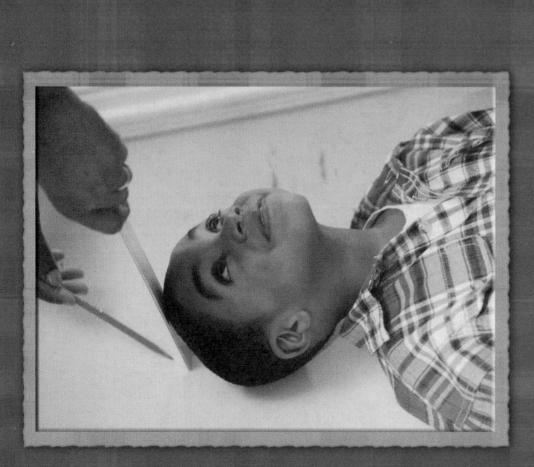

You can mark your height each year. You can see how much you have grown.

Name _____

Vocabulary

Match. Write the letter by the correct vocabulary word.

1. **inch** _____   **a.** a metric unit for measuring length

2. **quarter hour** _____   **b.** 15 minutes to an hour

3. **centimeter** _____   **c.** a customary unit for measuring length

Concepts

Find the object. Estimate. Then measure.

Find	Estimate	Measure
4.	about _____ inches	about _____ inches
5.	about _____ yards	about _____ yards
6.	about _____ feet	about _____ feet
7.	about _____ meters	about _____ meters
8. Dictionary	about _____ centimeters	about _____ centimeters

Draw the minute hand to show the time.

9.

`7:15`

10.

`12:30`

11.

`9:45`

Write how much time has passed for the activity.

Activity	Start Time	End Time	Time Passed
12.  We rode in a car.	: ___ ___	: ___ ___	We rode for _____ hours.

Circle the best unit to measure the time.

13. to clean my room

weeks   minutes

14. to sleep

hours   days

15. Trey and his mom went shopping. They left the house at 4:00 and did not get home until 6:00 at night. How long were they out shopping?

_____ hours

Summative Assessment

Name _____

Listen as your teacher reads each problem.
Choose the correct answer.

A Look at the picture of the pen. Measure the length of the pen and cap in inches. About how long are the pen and cap together?

○ about 1 inch   ○ about 2 inches
○ about 3 inches ○ about 4 inches

B Swimming lessons started at twelve o'clock P.M. and lasted two hours. At what time did the lessons end?

12:00 A.M.   2:00 P.M.
○   ○

3:00 P.M.   4:00 P.M.
○   ○

Listen as your teacher reads each problem.
Choose the correct answer.

1 Which unit would be best to measure the length of a book?

inches   feet
○   ○

yards   meters
○   ○

3 Camp starts at nine o'clock and ends seven hours later. What time does camp end?

7:00 P.M.   6:00 P.M.
○   ○

5:00 P.M.   4:00 P.M.
○   ○

2 This marker is about 4 cubes long. About how many paper clips long is the marker?

○ about 2 paper clips
○ about 3 paper clips
○ about 4 paper clips
○ about 5 paper clips

4 Look at the picture of the eraser. Measure the length of the eraser in centimeters. About how long is the eraser?

○ about 1 cm   ○ about 2 cm
○ about 3 cm   ○ about 5 cm

5 Which sign makes the number sentence true?

$$11 - 4 \boxed{} 7$$

> ○

< ○

− ○

= ○

8 Which can be used to check eighty-nine minus twenty-four equals sixty-five?

$$89 - 24 = 65$$

24 + 65 ○

89 + 65 ○

65 − 24 ○

24 + 89 ○

6 Look at the soup can. Which shape matches the soup can?

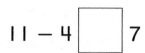

○　　○　　○　　○

9 Philip is going on vacation to visit his aunt and uncle. He will be gone for one month. About how long will Philip be gone?

60 minutes ○

7 days ○

30 days ○

365 days ○

7 What is the value of the five in five hundred thirty-two?

$$532$$

5 ○　　55 ○　　500 ○　　50 ○

10 Maude walked for one hour. How many minutes did Maude walk?

12 ○　　24 ○　　60 ○　　72 ○

Summative Assessment

STOP

Three-Digit Addition

Review Vocabulary
regroup

Explore

Look at the numbers on the seats. Do you see a pattern? Name the pattern you see.

Counting by_____.

Name _____

Are You Ready for Chapter 13?

Add.

1.   9
     + 8
     —

2.   8
     + 5
     —

3.   9
     + 1
     —

4.   71
    + 20
    —

5.   40
    + 30
    —

6.   56
    + 28
    —

7.   27¢
     + 33¢
     —

8. $0.71
    + 0.18
    —

9. $0.50
    + 0.25
    —

Round to the nearest **ten**.

10. 67 rounds to _____ .

11. 53 rounds to _____ .

12. 25 rounds to _____ .

13. 89 rounds to _____ .

14. Josefina eats about 20 peanuts a day. About
    how many peanuts will she eat in five days?

    about _____ peanuts

This page checks skills needed for Chapter 13

MATH at HOME

Dear Family,

Today my class started Chapter 13, **Three-Digit Addition**. In this chapter, I will learn to add three-digit numbers. Here is an activity we can do and a list of books we can read together.

Love,

_____

Activity

Have your child collect 10 items they can "sell" you. Place price tags ranging from 99¢ to $4.99 on each item. Have your child set up the store, and then pick two items at a time to purchase. For each sale, have your child write out the bill, including what was purchased and the price.

$3.74

Review Vocabulary

regroup to take apart a number to write it in a new way

regroup ⟶ 1
21
+ 19
――――
40

Math Online Click on the eGlossary at ca.gr2math.com to find out more about these words. There are 13 languages.

Books to Read

The Case of the Shrunken Allowance
by Joanne Rocklin
Cartwheel Books,
1999.

If You Hopped Like a Frog
by David Schwartz
Scholastic Press,
1999.

Mission: Addition
by Loreen Leedy
Holiday House, Inc.,
1999.

Estimada familia:

Hoy mi clase comenzó el Capítulo 13, **La suma con tres dígitos**. En este capítulo, aprenderé a sumar números de tres dígitos. A continuación, hay una actividad que podemos hacer y una lista de libros que podemos leer juntos.

Cariños,

_____

Actividad

Pídanle a su hijo(a) que reúna 10 artículos que pueda "venderles" a ustedes. Coloquen una etiqueta de precio en cada artículo que varíe de 99¢ a $4.99. Pídanle a su hijo(a) que arregle la tienda y, después, ustedes seleccionen dos artículos para comprar al mismo tiempo. Pídanle a su hijo(a) que escriba una factura para cada venta, la cual incluya lo comprado y el precio.

$3.74

Repaso de vocabulario

reagrupar separar un número para escribirlo de una nueva manera

$$
\text{reagrupar} \longrightarrow \begin{array}{r} 1 \\ 21 \\ + 19 \\ \hline 40 \end{array}
$$

Math Online Visiten el enlace eGlossary en ca.gr2math.com para averiguar más sobre estas palabras, las cuales se muestran en 13 idiomas.

Libros recomendados

El problema de cien libras
de Jennifer Dussling
The Kane Press, 2002.

Hacer decenas: grupos de gollyluvas
de John Burstein
Weekly Reader Early Learning Library, 2006.

Name _____

Add Hundreds

Get Ready

Main Idea

I will add numbers in the hundreds.

You can use addition facts to add numbers in the hundreds.

Find 300 + 400.

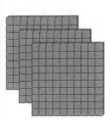

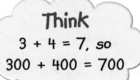
Think
3 + 4 = 7, so
300 + 400 = 700

$$\begin{array}{r} 3 \text{ hundreds} \\ + 4 \text{ hundreds} \\ \hline 7 \text{ hundreds} \end{array}$$ 300 + 400 = __700__

Check

Add.

1. 600 + 100 = _____

2. 300 + 300 = _____

3. 200 + 300 = _____

4. 700 + 200 = _____

5. 400 + 200 = _____

6. 800 + 100 = _____

7. $\begin{array}{r} 200 \\ + 100 \\ \hline \end{array}$

8. $\begin{array}{r} 100 \\ + 300 \\ \hline \end{array}$

9. $\begin{array}{r} 500 \\ + 0 \\ \hline \end{array}$

10. $\begin{array}{r} 400 \\ + 500 \\ \hline \end{array}$

11. **Talk About It** What addition fact can help you add 600 + 100?

Think...
of addition facts
you know.

Add.

12. 200 + 300 = _____

13. 400 + 400 = _____

14. 700 + 100 = _____

15. 600 + 300 = _____

16. 400 + 200 = _____

17. 100 + 100 = _____

18.   300
     + 400
     _____

19.   100
     + 800
     _____

20.   200
     + 600
     _____

21.   600
     + 300
     _____

22.   500
     + 300
     _____

23.   200
     + 700
     _____

24.   400
     + 300
     _____

25.   300
     + 200
     _____

26.   600
     + 200
     _____

27.   300
     + 100
     _____

28.   900
     +   0
     _____

29.   200
     + 200
     _____

Problem Solving

30. **Number Sense** Hanna has 700 pennies.
    Her brother gives her 200 more pennies.

    How many pennies does Hanna have?

    _____ pennies

    Write the addition fact that helped you to solve.

    _____ + _____ = _____

414   four hundred fourteen

Math at Home Activity: Ask your child how knowing
4 + 5 = 9 helps them to solve 400 + 500.

Name _____

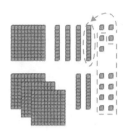
Regroup Ones

Get Ready

Main Idea

I will regroup the ones to add three-digit numbers.

Review Vocabulary

regroup

Find 135 + 328.

Step 1: Add the ones. If there are 10 or more ones, regroup 10 ones as 1 ten. Write the 1 in the tens column.

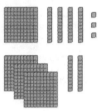

hundreds	tens	ones
	⋮1⋮	
1	3	5
+ 3	2	8
		3

Step 2: Add the tens.

hundreds	tens	ones
	⋮1⋮	
1	3	5
+ 3	2	8
	6	3

Step 3: Add the hundreds.

hundreds	tens	ones
	⋮1⋮	
1	3	5
+ 3	2	8
4	6	3

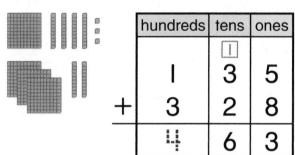

135 + 328 = 463

Check

Use base ten blocks and WorkMat 7. Add.

1. 436 + 245 = 681

2. 127 + 648 = _____

3.   651
   + 39

4.   521
   + 267

5.   349
   + 441

6.   315
   + 215

7. **Talk About It** How is three-digit addition like two-digit addition?

Use base ten blocks and WorkMat 7. Add.

8.   243
    + 219

9.   367
    + 516

10.   468
    + 23

11.   561
    + 26

12.   236
    + 518

13.   468
    + 18

14.   427
    + 144

15.   305
    + 306

Copy these problems on another piece of paper. Add.

16. 306 + 408 = _____

17. 28 + 515 = _____

18. 238 + 224 = _____

19. 607 + 13 = _____

20. 749 + 9 = _____

21. 146 + 253 = _____

H.O.T. Problem

22. **Make It Right** Josh adds 306 + 409 like this. Tell why Josh is wrong and make it right.

306
+ 409

70l5

_____

_____

_____

Math at Home Activity: Have your child show you how to add 477 + 413 and explain why regrouping is necessary.

Name _____

Add.

Color the sums that are < 600 yellow.
Color the sums that are > 600 orange.

1. 300
  + 200

2. 341
  + 216

3. 621
  +   4

4. 317
  + 438

5. 234
  + 436

6.   25
  + 274

7. 162
  + 519

8. 463
  + 27

9. 152
  + 208

10. 505
  + 206

11. 439
  + 53

12. 306
  + 539

Counting Up
Addition

You Will Need

- 30 ⚪ ⚫
- 🎲
- ♟
- pencil and paper

Play with a partner:

- Roll the 🎲 and move your ♟.
- Add the numbers.
- If the sum is > 500, take a counter.
- If the sum is < 500, take two counters.
- Play until both people reach Finish.
- The person with more counters wins.

START
```
  412
+  36
```
```
  126
+ 245
```
```
  355
+  26
```
```
  415
+ 165
```
```
   49
+ 123
```
```
  292
+ 206
```
```
  248
+ 236
```
```
  402
+  28
```
```
  105
+ 386
```
```
  218
+ 279
```
```
  129
+ 362
```
```
  258
+  23
```
```
  168
+ 328
```
```
  256
+ 205
```
FINISH
```
  104
+ 386
```
```
  107
+ 385
```

Name _____

Regroup Tens

Get Ready

Main Idea

I will regroup tens to add three-digit numbers.

Find 375 + 462.

Step 1: Add the ones.

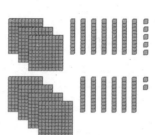

hundreds	tens	ones
3	7	5
+ 4	6	2
		7

Step 2: Add the tens. If there are 10 or more tens, regroup 10 tens as 1 hundred. Write the 1 in the hundreds column.

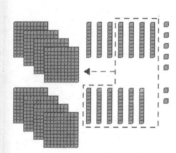

hundreds	tens	ones
1		
3	7	5
+ 4	6	2
	3	7

Step 3: Add the hundreds.

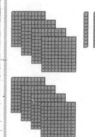

hundreds	tens	ones
1		
3	7	5
+ 4	6	2
8	3	7

375 + 462 = 837

Check

Use base ten blocks and WorkMat 7. Add.

1. 243 + 385 = 628

2. 562 + 174 = _____

3. 523
   + 93
   _____

4. 467
   + 61
   _____

5. 354
   + 53
   _____

6. 735
   + 192
   _____

7. **Talk About It** How is regrouping ones different from regrouping tens?

Use base ten blocks and WorkMat 7. Add.

8. 456 + 291	**9.** 732 + 167	**10.** 689 + 29	**11.** 485 + 332

12. 263 + 581	**13.** 586 + 1	**14.** 724 + 124	**15.** 446 + 60

Copy these problems on another piece of paper. Add.

16. $352 + 475 = $ _____

17. $389 + 51 = $ _____

18. $609 + 391 = $ _____

19. $559 + 300 = $ _____

20. $271 + 45 = $ _____

21. $654 + 251 = $ _____

Data File

One of the best ways to see all the amazing places in California is to travel by car or bus.

Miles to Cities in California

City	Oakland	Los Angeles	San Diego
Oakland		372	492
Los Angeles	372		122
San Diego	492	122	

22. Mia's family lives in Oakland. They drive to Los Angeles and then drive on to San Diego. How many miles do they drive on the trip?

_____ miles

Math at Home Activity: Ask your child to add $199 + 230$ and explain how he or she regrouped.

Name _____

Problem-Solving Strategy
Make a Table

Main Idea

I will make a table to solve problems.

Chris leaves for Hawaii at 2:30. Flights to Hawaii take off every two hours. Sonja is leaving 2 flights later. What time is Sonja's flight?

Understand

What do I know? Underline what you know.

What do I need to find? Circle the question.

Plan

How will I solve the problem?
I will make a table to find out what time Sonja will leave.

Solve

Make a table.

Sonja's plane will leave at _____ .

Flight	Time
1	2:30
2	4:30
3	

Check

Look Back
Did I answer the question?

Try It

Make a table to solve.

1. Our class collected food to donate. 20 cans were collected each day. How many cans were collected in 5 days?

_____ cans collected

2. Ryan gets to pass out papers to the class for 4 weeks. He uses 1 box of paper every week. There are 100 sheets of paper in a box. How many sheets of paper does he pass out?

_____ sheets of paper

Your Turn

Make a table to solve.

3. Marquis collects cars. He keeps 5 cars on a shelf. He has 4 shelves full of cars. How many cars does he have?

_____ cars

4. Lorraine wants to buy a birthday present for her brother. She saves a quarter every day. How much money will she have saved after 7 days?

_____

Math at Home Activity: Ask your child to explain his or her table for Exercise 4 to you.

Name _____

Add.

1. 400 + 400 = _____

2. 300 + 700 = _____

3. 600 + 200 = _____

4. 800 + 100 = _____

5. 300 + 200 = _____

6. 600 + 400 = _____

7. 500 + 100 = _____

8. 200 + 100 = _____

9. $\begin{array}{r} 422 \\ + 229 \\ \hline \end{array}$

10. $\begin{array}{r} 890 \\ + 17 \\ \hline \end{array}$

11. $\begin{array}{r} 844 \\ + 60 \\ \hline \end{array}$

12. $\begin{array}{r} 632 \\ + 175 \\ \hline \end{array}$

13. $\begin{array}{r} 514 \\ + 108 \\ \hline \end{array}$

14. $\begin{array}{r} 867 \\ + 21 \\ \hline \end{array}$

15. $\begin{array}{r} 651 \\ + 309 \\ \hline \end{array}$

16. $\begin{array}{r} 468 \\ + 215 \\ \hline \end{array}$

17. $\begin{array}{r} 187 \\ + 322 \\ \hline \end{array}$

18. $\begin{array}{r} 401 \\ + 182 \\ \hline \end{array}$

19. $\begin{array}{r} 771 \\ + 135 \\ \hline \end{array}$

20. $\begin{array}{r} 624 \\ + 4 \\ \hline \end{array}$

21. $\begin{array}{r} 399 \\ + 192 \\ \hline \end{array}$

22. $\begin{array}{r} 215 \\ + 684 \\ \hline \end{array}$

23. $\begin{array}{r} 468 \\ + 41 \\ \hline \end{array}$

24. $\begin{array}{r} 146 \\ + 76 \\ \hline \end{array}$

25. At the aquarium there are 368 fish in the tank. 260 starfish are put into the tank. Now how many fish and starfish are in the tank?

_____ fish and starfish

Spiral Review   Chapters 1–13

Add.

26.   35
       + 48

27.   29
       + 9

28.   64
       + 31

29.   30
       + 27

Round each addend to the nearest **ten.**
Estimate the sum.

30. 34 + 27

31. 66 + 21

_____ + _____ = _____   _____ + _____ = _____

Circle the two numbers in the ones column that add
to 10. Find the sum of the 3 numbers.

32.   3 1
       2 9
     + 4 0

33.   1 5
       2 5
     + 4 5

34.   6 2
         1
     + 1 8

35.   3 4
       1 6
     + 4 5

Write the number.

36. nine hundred eighteen _____

37. four hundred seven _____

Compare. Write >, <, or =.

38. 541 ◯ 145

39. 797 ◯ 977

---

40. Eric starts cleaning his room at 4:00. He is
finished at 6:00. How long did it take Eric to
clean his room?

_____ hours

Formative Assessment

Name _____

Estimate Sums

Main Idea

I will estimate the sums of three-digit numbers.

Estimate 429 + 267.

Webster School has 429 students. Jefferson school has 267 students. About how many students attend both schools?

You can estimate to find the answer.

Estimate to the nearest **ten.**	Estimate to the nearest **hundred.**
429 is closer to 430.	429 is closer to 400.
267 is closer to 270.	267 is closer to 300.

$$429 \xrightarrow{\text{rounds to}} 430$$
$$+267 \xrightarrow{\text{rounds to}} +270$$
$$700$$

$$429 \xrightarrow{\text{rounds to}} 400$$
$$+267 \xrightarrow{\text{rounds to}} +300$$
$$700$$

The number of students is about _700_.

The exact sum in 429 and 267 is 696.

Check

Estimate to the nearest **ten** and nearest **hundred**.
Then find the exact sum. Circle the closer estimate.

Exercise	Tens	Hundreds	Exact Sum
1. $\begin{array}{r} 385 \\ +517 \\ \hline \end{array}$	$+ \ \underline{}$	$+ \ \underline{}$	$\begin{array}{r} 385 \\ +517 \\ \hline 902 \end{array}$

2. **Talk About It** Explain why 500 is a better estimate than 400 for the sum of 391 + 102.

Estimate to the nearest **ten** and the nearest **hundred**.
Then find the exact sum. Circle the closer estimate.

Exercise	Tens	Hundreds	Exact Sum
3. 583 + 376	+ ___	+ ___	583 + 376
4. 246 + 212	+ ___	+ ___	246 + 212
5. 619 + 165	+ ___	+ ___	619 + 165
6. 625 + 355	+ ___	+ ___	625 + 355

7. **WRITING IN ▸MATH** Claire is having 350 people come to her big party. She told her mom she will need about 400 balloons. Will Claire have enough balloons for each person? _____

How do you know?

_____

_____

Math at Home Activity: Ask your child to estimate the sum of 102 and 910.

Name _____

Add Money

Main Idea

I will add money.

Sheila bought a bracelet for $4.25 and a scarf for $2.69. How much money did Sheila spend for the two items?

$$\begin{array}{r} \$4.25 \\ +\ 2.69 \\ \hline \$6.94 \end{array}$$

Sheila spent **$6.94**.

Remember
When you add money, you use a dollar sign and decimal point.

$4.25

$2.69

Check

Add.

1. $2.53
   + 3.27

2. $5.20
   + 3.80

3. $4.22
   + 1.38

4. $3.50
   + 3.70

5. $7.20
   + 2.51

6. $8.43
   + 0.64

7. $8.10
   + 1.90

8. $1.99
   + 3.90

9. $2.95 + $2.80 = _____

10. $6.00 + $1.70 = _____

11. **Talk About It** How are adding money and adding three-digit numbers alike?

Add.

12. $3.46
    + 4.34

13. $2.06
    + 4.96

14. $2.03
    + 1.93

15. $4.52
    + 5.08

16. $6.21
    + 2.29

17. $5.47
    + 1.23

18. $2.99
    + 1.25

19. $4.60
    + 3.40

20. $1.30
    + 0.70

21. $2.40
    + 3.50

22. $5.80
    + 2.99

23. $0.25
    + 2.70

24. $3.70
    + 3.30

25. $0.14
    + 3.70

26. $1.25
    + 8.00

Copy these problems on another piece of paper. Add.

27. $5.37 + $0.03 = _____

28. $6.55 + $1.35 = _____

29. $8.19 + $1.29 = _____

30. $7.99 + $1.10 = _____

Problem Solving

31. **Reasoning** Kent bought a baseball hat for $4.52 and two posters for $2.28 each. How much money did Kent spend?

_____

Math at Home Activity: Have your child add $7.90 and $2.10.

Name _____

Problem-Solving Investigation

Main Idea

I will choose a strategy to solve the problem.

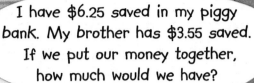

I have $6.25 saved in my piggy bank. My brother has $3.55 saved. If we put our money together, how much would we have?

Your Mission:
Find how much money Corey and his brother have altogether.

Understand

What do I know?
Underline what you know.
What do I need to find?
Circle it.

Plan

How will I solve the problem?
One way is to write a number sentence and find the sum.

Solve

I will write a number sentence.

Corey and his brother would have _____.

Check

Look back.
Does my answer solve the problem?

Mixed Problem Solving

Choose a strategy. Solve.

Problem-Solving Strategies

- Write a number sentence
- Use logical reasoning
- Make a table

1. Kendra puts three cars in a row.
   The black car is behind the red car.
   The red car is behind the white car.
   Which car is in front?

   _____ car

2. Tino's family went on vacation over the
   summer. If they traveled 312 miles to the
   beach, then 429 miles to his grandma's
   house, how many miles did they travel?

   _____ miles

3. For the school carnival, the principal needs to
   buy 505 bottles of water and 405 bottles of juice.
   There are 900 students. How many bottles will
   he buy?

   Will he have enough? _____

   _____ bottles

4. Ella gives out 3 packs of markers to each group.
   There are 5 groups in the class. How many
   packs of markers does Ella give out?

   _____ packs

430 four hundred thirty

Math at Home Activity: Take advantage of problem-solving
opportunities during daily routines such as riding in the car, bedtime,
doing laundry, putting away groceries, planning schedules, and so on.

You can attract butterflies to your yard. Just plant flowers they eat.

D

FOLD DOWN

Problem Solving in Science

Real-World MATH

Do you like butterflies? You can see butterflies in the summer.

This book belongs to

_____

A

Ricardo likes to keep track of how many butterflies he sees at the park each day.

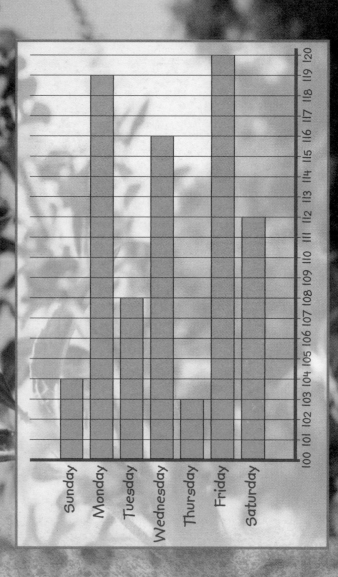

Use a pencil and paper. How many butterflies did Ricardo see on Sunday and Monday?

_____ butterflies

How many butterflies did Ricardo see on the last two days of the week?

_____ butterflies

Name _____

Vocabulary

Use the words below to complete the sentences.

| sum | addend | regroup | estimate |

1. In 1 + 2 = 3, the number 1 is called an _____.

2. When I don't need an exact answer, I can _____.

3. If the sum of the numbers in the ones column is ten or more, I will

   need to _____.

4. The answer to an addition sentence is the _____.

Concepts

Add.

5. 300 + 300 = _____

6. 200 + 800 = _____

7. 500 + 400 = _____

8. 600 + 200 = _____

9. 700 + 100 = _____

10. 300 + 200 = _____

11. 233
    + 549
    ‾‾‾‾‾

12. 428
    + 354
    ‾‾‾‾‾

13. 646
    + 148
    ‾‾‾‾‾

14. 555
    + 415
    ‾‾‾‾‾

15. 227
    + 13
    ‾‾‾‾‾

16. 319
    + 614
    ‾‾‾‾‾

17. 363
    + 181
    ‾‾‾‾‾

18. 395
    + 221
    ‾‾‾‾‾

Add.

19.
476
+ 231

20.
263
+ 556

21.
395
+ 129

22.
867
+ 51

23.
$2.25
+ 4.39

24.
$3.89
+ 6.04

25.
$7.77
+ 1.30

26.
$5.99
+ 0.50

Estimate to the nearest ten and nearest hundred.
Find the exact sum. Circle the closest estimate.

Exercise	Tens	Hundreds	Exact Sum
27. 573 + 146	+ ___	+ ___	573 + 146
28. 728 + 234	+ ___	+ ___	728 + 234

29. A fountain contains $7.65 in coins. Salvador
throws 4 more quarters into the fountain. How
much money does the fountain contain now?

_____

30. Jody estimates she has about 200 stickers.
She wants to have about 500 stickers in all. How
many more stickers does she need to collect?

about _____ stickers

Name _____

Listen as your teacher reads each problem.
Choose the correct answer.

A A computer room uses 300 sheets of paper in one month. The next month it uses 400. How many sheets of paper are used in all?

$$\begin{array}{r} 300 \\ + 400 \\ \hline \end{array}$$

100 ○   600 ○   700 ○   800 ○

B Look at the shapes. Which shape shows three-fourths?

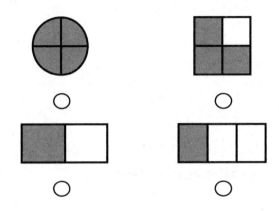

○   ○

○   ○

Listen as your teacher reads each problem.
Choose the correct answer.

1 What is the solution to this problem?

$$\begin{array}{r} 127 \\ + 77 \\ \hline \end{array}$$

404 ○   294 ○   284 ○   204 ○

3 What is the solution to this problem?

$$\begin{array}{r} 272 \\ + 189 \\ \hline \end{array}$$

500 ○   461 ○   451 ○   361 ○

2 Shane has 163 baseball cards. Robby has 208 baseball cards. How many baseball cards do they have altogether?

Shane	163
Robby	208

471 ○   461 ○   371 ○   361 ○

4 Look at the pencil and the ruler below it. What is the length of the pencil to the nearest inch?

○ 5 inches   ○ 3 inches

○ 6 inches   ○ 4 inches

5 Which number goes in the box?

$$30 < \boxed{} < 60$$

14   22   42   71
○   ○   ○   ○

6 What number goes in the box to make this number sentence true?

$$4 + 5 = \boxed{} + 4$$

3   4   5   6
○   ○   ○   ○

7 Marla did this subtraction problem. Which addition problem shows that she got the right answer?

$$\begin{array}{r} 81 \\ - 27 \\ \hline 54 \end{array}$$

54	51	59	27
+ 27	+ 31	+ 31	+ 20
81	20	28	7
○	○	○	○

8 A number has six ones, eight tens, and three hundreds What is the number?

286   386   468   683
○   ○   ○   ○

9 Round each addend to the nearest hundred. Add the hundreds to estimate the sum.

$$333 + 569$$

900   800   700   600
○   ○   ○   ○

10 Look at the shapes. Which shape is a cone?

○   ○

○   ○

STOP

Summative Assessment

Three-Digit Subtraction

Review Vocabulary

subtract

regroup

estimate

Explore

Elephants can live up to 80 years. Estimate how old these elephants are:

_____, _____, _____

Are You Ready for Chapter 14?

Subtract.

1.
$$\begin{array}{r} 9 \\ -\ 6 \\ \hline \end{array}$$

2.
$$\begin{array}{r} 8 \\ -\ 8 \\ \hline \end{array}$$

3.
$$\begin{array}{r} 17 \\ -\ 8 \\ \hline \end{array}$$

4.
$$\begin{array}{r} 14 \\ -\ 5 \\ \hline \end{array}$$

5.
$$\begin{array}{r} 60 \\ -\ 30 \\ \hline \end{array}$$

6.
$$\begin{array}{r} 83 \\ -\ 57 \\ \hline \end{array}$$

7.
$$\begin{array}{r} 62¢ \\ -\ 37¢ \\ \hline \end{array}$$

8.
$$\begin{array}{r} 72¢ \\ -\ 25¢ \\ \hline \end{array}$$

9.
$$\begin{array}{r} \$0.95 \\ -\ 0.14 \\ \hline \end{array}$$

10.
$$\begin{array}{r} \$0.09 \\ -\ 0.06 \\ \hline \end{array}$$

11.
$$\begin{array}{r} \$0.81 \\ -\ 0.68 \\ \hline \end{array}$$

12.
$$\begin{array}{r} \$0.43 \\ -\ 0.25 \\ \hline \end{array}$$

Round to the nearest hundred.

13. 892 rounds to _____.

14. 422 rounds to _____.

15. 917 rounds to _____.

16. 355 rounds to _____.

17. Rick saw eight squirrels. Two ran away.
How many squirrels does Rick see now?

_____ squirrels

This page checks skills needed for Chapter 14.

MATH at HOME

Dear Family,

Today my class started Chapter 14, **Three-Digit Subtraction**. In this chapter, I will learn to subtract three-digit numbers. Here is an activity we can do and a list of books we can read together.

Love,

_____

Activity

Phone Book

Give your child a list of phone numbers of friends and family in different locations. Have your child find the differences between your area code and those on the list. Subtract the smaller area code from the larger area code each time.

Review Vocabulary

subtract to take away, take apart, separate, or find the difference between two sets; the opposite of add

regroup to take apart a number to write it in a new way

    1 ten 2 ones becomes 12 ones

estimate to find a number close to an exact amount

Math Online Click on the eGlossary link at ca.gr2math.com to find out more about these words. There are 13 languages.

Books to Read

The Water Hole
by Graeme Base
Harry N. Abrams, 2001.

Panda Math: Learning About Subtraction from Hua Mei and Mei Sheng
by Ann Whitehead Nagda Henry Holt and Co., 2005.

Alexander, Who Used to Be Rich Last Sunday
by Judith Viorst
Aladdin, 1987.

MATEMÁTICAS en CASA

Estimada familia:

Hoy mi clase comenzó el Capítulo 14, **La resta con tres dígitos.** En este capítulo, aprenderé a restar números de tres dígitos. A continuación, hay una actividad que podemos hacer y una lista de libros que podemos leer juntos.

Cariños,

_____

Actividad

Phone Book

Denle a su hijo(a) una lista de números telefónicos de familiares y amigos en diferentes lugares. Pídanle que busque las diferencias entre su código de área y los de la lista. En cada oportunidad, resten el código de área menor del código de área mayor.

Vocabulario clave

restar quitar, separar o hallar la diferencia entre dos conjuntos; lo opuesto de la adición

reagrupar separar un número para escribirlo de una nueva manera
   1 decena 2 unidades se convierten en 12 unidades

estimar hallar un número cercano a una cantidad exacta

Math Online Visiten el enlace eGlossary en ca.gr2math.com para averiguar más sobre estas palabras, las cuales se muestran en 13 idiomas.

Libros recomendados

Alexander que era rico el domingo pasado
de Judith Viorst
Simon & Schuster Children's Publishing, 1989.

La charca
de Graeme Base
Ediciones Omega, 2003.

440 four hundred forty

Name _____

Subtract Hundreds

Main Idea

I will subtract numbers in the hundreds.

Review Vocabulary

subtract

You can use subtraction facts to subtract the hundreds.

Find 500 − 300.

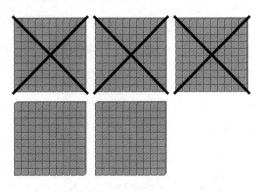

Think
I know 5 − 3 = 2, so 500 − 300 = 200.

$$\begin{array}{r} 5 \text{ hundreds} \\ -\ 3 \text{ hundreds} \\ \hline 2 \text{ hundreds} \end{array}$$

$500 - 300 = \underline{200}$

✔ Check

Subtract.

1. $800 - 100 = \underline{700}$

2. $200 - 200 = \underline{}$

3. $600 - 500 = \underline{}$

4. $900 - 400 = \underline{}$

5. $\begin{array}{r} 700 \\ -\ 100 \\ \hline \end{array}$

6. $\begin{array}{r} 400 \\ -\ 200 \\ \hline \end{array}$

7. $\begin{array}{r} 500 \\ -\ \ \ 0 \\ \hline \end{array}$

8. $\begin{array}{r} 700 \\ -\ 300 \\ \hline \end{array}$

9. **Talk About It** What subtraction fact can you use to find 900 − 800?

Use the subtraction facts you know to solve these.

Subtract.

10. 800 − 300 = _____

11. 600 − 600 = _____

12. 300 − 100 = _____

13. 900 − 200 = _____

14. 800 − 400 = _____

15. 700 − 500 = _____

16.
```
   700
 − 400
 ─────
```

17.
```
   800
 − 200
 ─────
```

18.
```
   300
 − 300
 ─────
```

19.
```
   500
 − 400
 ─────
```

20.
```
   500
 − 300
 ─────
```

21.
```
   200
 − 100
 ─────
```

22.
```
   600
 − 200
 ─────
```

23.
```
   900
 − 700
 ─────
```

24.
```
   700
 − 200
 ─────
```

25.
```
   400
 − 300
 ─────
```

26.
```
   800
 −   0
 ─────
```

27.
```
   800
 − 800
 ─────
```

H.O.T. Problems

When you subtract a number that is 1 less than the first number, the difference is 1.
For example, 5 − 4 = 1 or 500 − 499 = 1.

28. 400 − 399 = _____

29. 701 − 700 = _____

30. 601 − 600 = _____

31. 300 − 299 = _____

32. 501 − 500 = _____

33. 600 − 599 = _____

Math at Home Activity: Ask your child what number is 100 less than 500.

Name _____

Regroup Tens

Get Ready

Main Idea

I will regroup tens to subtract three-digit numbers.

Review Vocabulary

regroup

Find 652 − 429.

Step 1: Subtract the ones. You cannot subtract 9 from 2. Regroup 1 ten as 10 ones.

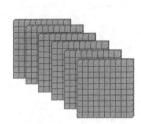 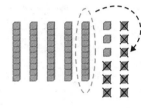

hundreds	tens	ones
6	4̶5̶	1̶2̶
− 4	2	9
		3

Step 2: Subtract the tens.

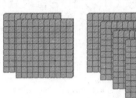

hundreds	tens	ones
6	4̶5̶	1̶2̶
− 4	2	9
	2	3

Step 3: Subtract the hundreds.

hundreds	tens	ones
6	4̶5̶	1̶2̶
− 4	2	9
2	2	3

652 − 429 = __223__

Check

Use base ten blocks and WorkMat 7. Subtract.

1. 546 − 17 = _____

2. 782 − 439 = _____

3. 965 − 327 = _____

4. 450 − 8 = _____

5. **Talk About It** How is subtracting three-digit numbers like subtracting two-digit numbers?

> **Practice**

Use base ten blocks and WorkMat 7. Subtract.

6. 382 − 128 = _____

7. 467 − 49 = _____

8. 691 − 233 = _____

9. 575 − 66 = _____

10. 863 − 18 = _____

11. 754 − 507 = _____

12.   455
      − 325

13.   780
      − 436

14.   652
      − 35

15.   931
      −   6

Copy these problems on another piece of paper. Subtract.

16.   742
      − 219

17.   423
      − 119

18. 550 − 307 = _____

19. 762 − 56 = _____

20. 471 − 315 = _____

21. 893 − 246 = _____

H.O.T. Problem

22. **Make it Right** Ana subtracted 381 − 165 like this. Tell why Ana is wrong. Make it right.

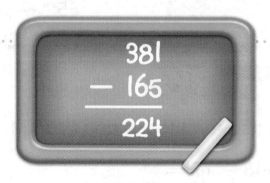

381
− 165
224

Math at Home Activity: Write this problem on a piece of paper: 618 − 309. Have your child subtract.

Name _____

Subtract.

1.
729
− 317
_____

2.
928
− 18
_____

3.
423
− 116
_____

4.
582
− 264
_____

5.
662
− 329
_____

6.
835
− 427
_____

7.
475
− 25
_____

8.
846
− 639
_____

9.
330
− 3
_____

10.
488
− 119
_____

11.
689
− 425
_____

12.
397
− 141
_____

Subtract It!
Subtraction

What you need:

Play with a partner:

○ Take turns. Roll the . Put your ♟ on that flower.

○ Subtract. If you are right, put ◯ on the flower.

○ Move your ♟ to each flower only once.

○ The first person to "pick" all of the flowers wins!

1. 332
   − 110

2. 200
   − 100

3. 476
   − 228

4. 651
   − 170

5. 700
   − 200

6. 591
   − 47

Name _____

Regroup Hundreds

Get Ready

Main Idea

I will regroup hundreds to subtract three-digit numbers.

Find 539 − 285.

Step 1: Subtract the ones.

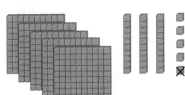

hundreds	tens	ones
5	3	9
− 2	8	5
		4

Step 2: Subtract the tens. You cannot subtract 8 from 3. Regroup 1 hundred as 10 tens. Now subtract the tens.

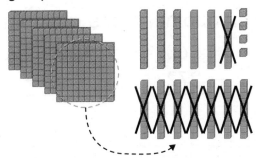

hundreds	tens	ones
4	13	
5̶	3̶	9
− 2	8	5
	5	4

Step 3: Subtract the hundreds.

hundreds	tens	ones
4	13	
5̶	3̶	9
− 2	8	5
2	5	4

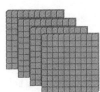

539 − 285 = 254

Check

Use base ten blocks and WorkMat 7. Subtract.

1. 568 − 197 = _____

2. 628 − 442 = _____

3. 759 − 5 = _____

4. 341 − 22 = _____

5. **Talk About It** How do you know when to regroup?

Practice

Use base ten blocks and WorkMat 7. Subtract.

6. 586 − 295 = _____

7. 638 − 43 = _____

8. 929 − 777 = _____

9. 457 − 29 = _____

10. 799 − 541 = _____

11. 870 − 433 = _____

12.
```
   545
 − 362
```

13.
```
   638
 −  36
```

14.
```
   232
 − 170
```

15.
```
   948
 − 472
```

Copy these problems on another piece of paper. Subtract.

16.
```
   827
 − 247
```

17.
```
   565
 − 272
```

18.
```
   640
 −  50
```

19.
```
   729
 − 135
```

Data File

In 1863, workers started building a railroad in California going east. In the east, people started building a track going west. After six years, the two tracks met.

20. It took 227 days to build railroad tracks over a mountain. It took 132 days to build tracks on flat ground. How many more days did it take to build over the mountain?

_____ days

Math at Home Activity: Have your child show how to find 641 − 387 and explain the regrouping.

Name _____

Problem-Solving Strategy
Guess and Check

Main Idea

I will guess and check to solve a problem.

Dan has two baskets of apples. He has 80 apples in all. How many apples might be in each basket?
Use the numbers below to help you.

25   35   45   56

Understand

What do I know? Underline what you know.

What do I need to find? Circle the question.

Plan

How will I solve the problem?

I will make a guess. Then I will check my answer.

Solve

Use guess and check to solve.

$$25 + 35 = 60$$

First try: too low

$$45 + 56 = 101$$

Second try: too high

$$35 + 45 = 80$$

Third try: correct. So, Dan has 35 apples in one basket and 45 in the other.

Check

Look back.

Did I answer the question?

Try It

Remember
Understand
Plan
Solve
Check

Guess and check to solve.

1. The sum of two numbers is 75.
   One number is 5 less than the other.
   Circle the two numbers.

   15   20   35   40   65

2. Maggie has 10 coins that equal 64¢. She has
   more dimes than quarters, more nickels than
   dimes, and more pennies than nickels. What
   coins could Maggie have?

Your Turn

Guess and check to solve.

3. Lauren's toy race cars are two different colors.
   She has 36 cars in all. Which two colors are her cars?

   red 10   green 16   blue 20

4. What number am I?
   I am more than 143 + 137.
   I have a 9 in the tens place.
   The sum of my digits is 14.
   Look at the numbers below.
   Circle the number.

   204   268   340   392   399

450   four hundred fifty

Math at Home Activity: Ask your child to explain
how he or she solved Exercise 4.

Name _____

Subtract.

1. 800 − 500 = _____

2. 500 − 300 = _____

3. 900 − 200 = _____

4. 700 − 300 = _____

5. 863 − 347 = _____

6. 253 − 39 = _____

7. 655 − 227 = _____

8. 527 − 19 = _____

9. 553
  − 306
  _____

10. 770
  − 642
  _____

11. 483
  − 34
  _____

12. 853
  − 149
  _____

13. 475
  − 295
  _____

14. 647
  − 382
  _____

15. 954
  −   7
  _____

16. 827
  − 683
  _____

17. 319
  − 29
  _____

18. 444
  − 282
  _____

19. 875
  − 481
  _____

20. 206
  − 11
  _____

21. There are 620 buttons in a box. 200 of them
    are square. 40 of them are heart-shaped. The
    rest are round. How many round buttons are
    in the box?

_____ round buttons

Count on to add.

22. 5 + 2 = _____   **23.** 7 + 1 = _____   **24.** 3 + 5 = _____

Finish the tally chart. Answer the questions.

After-School Activites		
Activity	Tally	Total
Homework	ЖТ ЖТ	
Football	ЖТ I	
Park	ЖТ III	
Bike Riding	II	

25. How many students said homework?

_____ students

26. How many students said bike riding or football?

_____ students

Round each number to the nearest **ten.**
Estimate the difference.

27. 31 − 18

_____ − _____ = _____

28. 42 − 14

_____ − _____ = _____

29. 45 − 19

_____ − _____ = _____

30. 49 − 31

_____ − _____ = _____

Circle the shapes that match the description.

31. 4 sides and 4 vertices

32. 3 sides and 3 vertices

Formative Assessment

Name _____

Estimate Differences

Main Idea

I will estimate the difference of three-digit numbers.

Review Vocabulary

estimate

It is 357 miles from Anaheim to Phoenix and 266 miles from Anaheim to Las Vegas. About how many more miles is it from Anaheim to Phoenix?

You can estimate to find the answer.

Estimate to the nearest **ten**.	Estimate to the nearest **hundred**.
357 is closer to 360.	357 is closer to 400.
266 is closer to 270.	266 is closer to 300.

$$
\begin{array}{r} 357 \\ -\ 266 \\ \end{array} \xrightarrow{\text{rounds to}} \begin{array}{r} 360 \\ -\ 270 \\ \hline 90 \end{array}
$$

About __90__ miles

$$
\begin{array}{r} 357 \\ -\ 266 \\ \end{array} \xrightarrow{\text{rounds to}} \begin{array}{r} 400 \\ -\ 300 \\ \hline 100 \end{array}
$$

About __100__ miles

The exact difference in 357 and 266 is 91 miles. So, both estimates are reasonable.

Check

Estimate to the nearest **ten** and nearest **hundred**. Then find the exact difference. Circle the closer estimate.

	Exercise	Tens	Hundreds	Exact Difference
1.	$\begin{array}{r} 482 \\ -\ 217 \\ \hline \end{array}$	$\begin{array}{r} 480 \\ -\ 220 \\ \hline 260 \end{array}$	$-$	$\begin{array}{r} 482 \\ -\ 217 \\ \hline 265 \end{array}$

2. **Talk About It** Estimate 789 to the nearest ten and hundred. Explain how the answers are different.

Estimate to the nearest **ten** and nearest **hundred**.
Then find the exact difference. Circle the closer estimate.

Exercise	Tens	Hundreds	Exact Difference
3. 762 − 308			762 − 308
4. 982 − 273			982 − 273
5. 423 − 357			423 − 357
6. 870 − 431			870 − 431

7. **WRITING IN ►MATH** In New York City, the
Empire State Building is 381 meters tall, and
the Trump Tower is 202 meters tall. Dion
estimated the difference in heights to be 180
meters. Chris estimated the difference to be
200 meters. Why are their estimates different?

_____

_____

What is the exact difference in the heights? _____ meters

Math at Home Activity: Ask your child to round 923 and 210 to the
nearest ten, and then subtract. Repeat the activity rounding to the nearest
hundred.

Name _____

Subtract Money

Main Idea

I will subtract money.

The girls earn $7.70 planting trees.
The next day they earn $8.50 walking dogs.
How much more money did they
earn walking dogs?

```
      7  15
$8 . 5 0
-  7 . 7 0
----------
$0 . 8 0
```

Check

Subtract.

1. $6.43
  − 3.25
  _____
  $3.18

2. $4.25
  − 2.82

3. $7.29
  − 2.48

4. $5.46
  − 3.27

5. $9.53
  − 6.71

6. $8.79
  − 0.75

7. $2.50
  − 1.19

8. $7.99
  − 1.00

9. **Talk About It** How is subtracting three-digit numbers
and subtracting money different?

Subtract.

Remember
Use a dollar sign and decimal point when subtracting money.

10. $7.43
    − 5.34

11. $8.52
    − 3.07

12. $6.29
    − 2.32

13. $5.74
    − 1.68

14. $3.50
    − 2.70

15. $7.99
    − 0.50

16. $9.97
    − 1.51

17. $9.20
    − 1.40

18. $3.36
    − 1.42

19. $5.96
    − 0.18

20. $6.18
    − 2.64

Copy these problems on another piece of paper.
Subtract.

21. $4.25
    − 0.75

22. $4.70
    − 3.80

23. $6.70
    − 0.52

24. $3.75
    − 2.66

Problem Solving

25. **Number Sense** Subtract the amounts of money.
    Which difference is the greatest amount? Circle it.

    $6.23
    − 2.54

    $4.62
    − 1.77

    $6.25
    − 2.37

26. Explain how you know which amount is greatest.

_____

_____

Math at Home Activity: Look at two different prices at the grocery store, up to $10.00. Have your child subtract the greater price from the lesser price.

Name _____

Problem-Solving Investigation

Main Idea

I will choose a strategy to solve the problem.

Your Mission:
Find how many cubes she started with.

I gave Polly 200 cubes. I gave Rikki 100 cubes. I have 300 cubes left. How many cubes did I start with?

Understand

What do I know? Underline what you know.
What do I need to find? Circle it.

Plan

How will I solve the problem?
One way is to work backward.

Solve

Work backward.

| Polly has 200 cubes. | Rikki has 100 cubes. | I have 300 cubes. | $300 + 100 = \underline{400}$ |
| | | | $400 + 200 = \underline{600}$ |

I started with __600__ cubes.

Check

Look Back
Does my answer make sense?
How can I check my answer?

Mixed Problem Solving

Problem-Solving Strategies

- Work backward
- Find a pattern
- Use logical reasoning

Choose a strategy. Solve.

1. I am a number greater than 100.
   There is a two in the ones place.
   I am less than 104.
   What number am I?

   _____

2. Bailey gave her brother $1.00. Now she has
   $3.27. How much money did Bailey have to
   begin with?

   _____

3. Brooke needs to put 2 fish in each bowl
   for a game at the school fair. She has
   17 bowls. How many fish does she need?

   _____ fish

4. My lunch costs $1.50. Each item costs
   the same. How much does each item cost?
   Do I have enough money?

   _____; _____

 Math at Home Activity: Take advantage of problem-solving
opportunities during daily routines such as riding in the car, bedtime,
doing laundry, putting away groceries, planning schedules, and so on.

A farmer in Fresno, California, is sending his tomatoes to three different cities. The table shows how far the trucks will travel.

City	Miles
Las Vegas, NV	396
Flagstaff, AZ	593
Phoenix, AZ	591

One truck travels to Las Vegas. Another truck travels to Phoenix. Which truck travels farther?

The truck going to _____ .

FOLD DOWN

D

Problem Solving in Social Sciences

Real-World MATH

Do you know what happens to vegetables before they are ready to eat?

_____

This book belongs to

_____

A

They are loaded onto big trucks. Some vegetables are sent to be canned, and some are sent to be frozen.

Some vegetables are sent to the grocery store.

Farmers grow some vegetables from seeds. Then the vegetables are picked.

Name _____

Vocabulary

Draw a line to match each term with an example.

1. decimal point

2. subtract

3. round

a. $3 - 2 = 1$

b. $432 \longrightarrow \mathbf{400}$

c. $5.79

Concepts

Subtract.

4. $600 - 400 =$ _____

5. $700 - 600 =$ _____

6.
$$\begin{array}{r} 800 \\ -\ 400 \\ \hline \end{array}$$

7.
$$\begin{array}{r} 900 \\ -\ 600 \\ \hline \end{array}$$

8.
$$\begin{array}{r} 773 \\ -\ 559 \\ \hline \end{array}$$

9.
$$\begin{array}{r} 261 \\ -\ 148 \\ \hline \end{array}$$

10.
$$\begin{array}{r} 938 \\ -\ 329 \\ \hline \end{array}$$

11.
$$\begin{array}{r} 885 \\ -\ 618 \\ \hline \end{array}$$

12.
$$\begin{array}{r} 357 \\ -\ 185 \\ \hline \end{array}$$

13.
$$\begin{array}{r} 987 \\ -\ 596 \\ \hline \end{array}$$

14.
$$\begin{array}{r} 446 \\ -\ 171 \\ \hline \end{array}$$

15.
$$\begin{array}{r} 663 \\ -\ 273 \\ \hline \end{array}$$

16.
$$\begin{array}{r} 399 \\ -\ 12 \\ \hline \end{array}$$

17.
$$\begin{array}{r} 516 \\ -\ 7 \\ \hline \end{array}$$

18.
$$\begin{array}{r} \$4.25 \\ -\ 3.09 \\ \hline \end{array}$$

19.
$$\begin{array}{r} \$8.77 \\ -\ 2.94 \\ \hline \end{array}$$

20.
$$\begin{array}{r} \$5.86 \\ -\ 1.37 \\ \hline \end{array}$$

21.
$$\begin{array}{r} \$8.04 \\ -\ 0.91 \\ \hline \end{array}$$

Estimate to the nearest **ten** and **nearest** hundred.
Then find the exact difference. Circle the closer estimate.

Exercise	Tens	Hundreds	Exact Difference
22. $\begin{array}{r} 759 \\ -\ 334 \\ \hline \end{array}$			$\begin{array}{r} 759 \\ -\ 334 \\ \hline \end{array}$
23. $\begin{array}{r} 887 \\ -\ 718 \\ \hline \end{array}$			$\begin{array}{r} 887 \\ -\ 718 \\ \hline \end{array}$
24. $\begin{array}{r} 546 \\ -\ 475 \\ \hline \end{array}$			$\begin{array}{r} 546 \\ -\ 475 \\ \hline \end{array}$
25. $\begin{array}{r} 802 \\ -\ 466 \\ \hline \end{array}$			$\begin{array}{r} 802 \\ -\ 466 \\ \hline \end{array}$

26. A box of cereal costs $3.59 at the grocery store. Samuel gives the cashier $5.75. How much change should Samuel get back?

_____

27. There were 334 cars in the mall parking lot on Sunday. On Monday, there were 182 cars in the same lot. How many more cars were parked in the lot on Sunday?

_____

Summative Assessment

Name _____

Listen as your teacher reads each problem.
Choose the correct answer.

A In one week, the Mann Company collected eight hundred pounds of tin. They also collected four hundred pounds of plastic. How much more tin did they collect than plastic?

$$\begin{array}{r} 800 \\ -\ 400 \\ \hline \end{array}$$

500   400   300   200
○   ○   ○   ○

B Jorge's coloring book has three hundred twenty-one pages. He has colored one hundred seventeen pages. How many pages does he have left to color?

$$\begin{array}{r} 321 \\ -\ 117 \\ \hline \end{array}$$

94   104   154   204
○   ○   ○   ○

Listen as your teacher reads each problem.
Choose the correct answer.

1 What is another name for five hundred plus fifty plus one?

500501 ○   5051 ○

5501 ○   551 ○

3
$$\begin{array}{r} 156 \\ -\ 95 \\ \hline \end{array}$$

60   61   65   251
○   ○   ○   ○

2 I have two hundred fifty-four stamps in my collection. I gave one hundred thirty-six stamps to my brother. How many stamps do I have left?

$$\begin{array}{r} 254 \\ -\ 136 \\ \hline \end{array}$$

128   124   118   108
○   ○   ○   ○

4 Terry put eighteen photos into three equal groups. How many photos are in each group?

5   6   7   8
○   ○   ○   ○

5 Which number will make this sentence true?

$$512 < \underline{\hspace{1.5cm}}$$

367   498   502   539

○   ○   ○   ○

---

6 Which number goes in the box?

$$93 < \boxed{} < 99$$

100   94   92   91

○   ○   ○   ○

---

7 Look at the circle. What fraction of the circle is shaded?

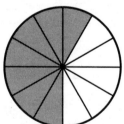

$\dfrac{7}{12}$ $\dfrac{6}{12}$ $\dfrac{5}{12}$ $\dfrac{4}{12}$

○   ○   ○   ○

---

8 What is the solution to this problem?

$$\begin{array}{r} 678 \\ - 21 \\ \hline \end{array}$$

750   657   457   375

○   ○   ○   ○

---

9 About how long is a dollar bill?

1 centimeter   1 inch

○   ○

6 meters   6 inches

○   ○

---

10 What is the difference between the tallest height and the shortest height?

Tree Height	
maple	109 feet
pine	344 feet
oak	572 feet

360   400   460   463

○   ○   ○   ○

STOP

Summative Assessment

Standards Review

It's time to review the California Mathematics Standards. You have been building your math skills in class. Soon you will have a chance to put them to work.

Tips for Success!

Before a Test

- Go to bed early the night before.
- Eat a good breakfast the next morning.

During a Test

- Listen carefully as your teacher reads each question.
- Work carefully.

Whatever you do...

- Do not rush.
- Do not give up.

RELAX.
Just do your best.

Bubbles

You will fill in bubbles to answer questions.

Make sure to:

• Fill in the bubble completely.

• Make your marks dark.

• If you make a mistake, erase it all.

Correct			
2	5	7	9
⬭	⬭	⬬	⬭

Not Correct			
2	5	7	9
⬭	⬭	⊙	⬭

Not Correct			
2	5	7	9
⬭	⬭	⊗	⬭

Not Correct			
2	5	7	9
⬭	⬭	◎	⬭

Not Correct			
2	5	7	9
⬭	⬭	✓	⬭

Name _____

Practice by Standard: Number Sense

Standard Set 1.0: Students understand the relationship between numbers, quantities, and place value in whole numbers up to 1,000.

Directions

Listen as your teacher reads each problem.
Choose the correct answer.

QUICK Practice

1. What is another way to write seven hundred fifty-three?

   ○ 700 + 50 + 30

   ○ 700 + 53 + 3

   ○ 700 + 50 + 3

   ○ 500 + 70 + 3

QUICK Review

Strategy: Write seven hundred fifty-three in expanded form.

There is a 7 in the hundreds place.

There is a 5 in the tens place.

There is a 3 in the ones place.

How can you write this number?

---

2. A number has four ones, seven tens, and six hundreds. What is the number?

   476   647   674   764
   ○   ○   ○   ○

Strategy: Use place value to form a whole number.

The table below shows the correct place values of the digits.

hundreds	tens	ones
6	7	4

Copyright © Macmillan/McGraw-Hill, a division of The McGraw-Hill Companies, Inc.

California Standards Review **CA3**

Practice On Your Own

Directions
Listen as your teacher reads each problem.
Choose the correct answer.

3. What is the value of the eight in three hundred thirty-eight?

    8   80   800   8,000

    ○   ○   ○   ○

4. What is another name for seven hundred plus sixty plus five?

  765 7,056 7,065 70,650

    ○   ○   ○   ○

5. Which number goes in the box?

    418   508   522   569

    ○   ○   ○   ○

6. Which sign makes the number sentence true?

    $30 + 14 \;\boxed{}\; 44$

    +   >   <   =

    ○   ○   ○   ○

7. A number has two ones, nine tens, and three hundreds. What is the number?

    139   193   319   392

    ○   ○   ○   ○

8. Which number sentence is true?

  456 < 456   219 > 233

      ○   ○

  540 > 543   763 < 770

      ○   ○

9. What is the value of the two in two hundred seventy-four?

    2   20   200   2,000

    ○   ○   ○   ○

10. Which number goes in the box?

    308   357   399   412

    ○   ○   ○   ○

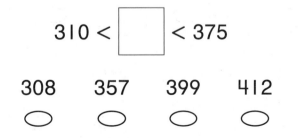

Name _____

Practice by Standard: Number Sense

Standard Set 2.0: Students estimate, calculate, and solve problems involving addition and subtraction of two- and three-digit numbers.

Directions
Listen as your teacher reads each problem.
Choose the correct answer.

QUICK Practice

1. Lawrence did this subtraction problem. Which addition problem shows that he got the right answer?

$$\begin{array}{r} 37 \\ -\ 24 \\ \hline 13 \end{array}$$

$$\begin{array}{r} 13 \\ +\ 24 \\ \hline \end{array}$$ $$\begin{array}{r} 24 \\ +\ 24 \\ \hline \end{array}$$ $$\begin{array}{r} 13 \\ +\ 37 \\ \hline \end{array}$$ $$\begin{array}{r} 37 \\ +\ 24 \\ \hline \end{array}$$

○   ○   ○   ○

2. What is the solution to this problem?

$$\begin{array}{r} 119 \\ +\ \ 33 \\ \hline \end{array}$$

142   149   152   157

○   ○   ○   ○

QUICK Review

Strategy: Add to check a subtraction problem.

Add the difference (13) to the number subtracted (24). The sum should equal 37.

$$\begin{array}{r} 37 \\ -\ 24 \\ \hline 13 \end{array} \qquad \begin{array}{r} 13 \\ +\ 24 \\ \hline 37 \end{array}$$

Strategy: Use regrouping to solve an addition problem.

Add the digits in the ones column. $9 + 3 = 12$
The sum is 10 or more, so you regroup. Regroup 12 as 1 ten and 2 ones. Write the ones. Then add the tens and hundreds.

Practice On Your Own

Directions
Listen as your teacher reads each problem.
Choose the correct answer.

3. What is the solution to this problem?

$$\begin{array}{r} 438 \\ -\ \ 35 \\ \hline \end{array}$$

401 403 413 417
○   ○   ○   ○

4. Michelle had three hundred sixty-eight stickers. She gave one hundred forty-two of them to her friends. How many stickers does Michelle have left?

194   208   216   226
○   ○   ○   ○

5. Estimate to find the answer to the problem in the box.

about 10   about 20
○   ○

about 30   about 40
○   ○

6. Which of these can be used to check the answer to the problem in the box?

$$\boxed{20 - 11 = 9}$$

$9 + 11 = 20$ $11 + 11 = 22$
○   ○

$20 + 9 = 29$ $20 - 8 = 12$
○   ○

7. Antonio scored eighteen points in his first basketball game. He scored twenty-one points in his second game. About how many points did he score altogether?

about 20   about 40
○   ○

about 50   about 60
○   ○

8. What is the solution to this problem?

$$\begin{array}{r} 146 \\ -\ \ 61 \\ \hline \end{array}$$

85   82   73   65
○   ○   ○   ○

Name _____

Practice by Standard: Number Sense

Standard Set 3.0: Students model and solve simple problems involving multiplication and division.

Directions
Listen as your teacher reads each problem.
Choose the correct answer.

1. Which drawing shows three times four?

$$3 \times 4$$

Strategy: Use repeated addition to model multiplication. How many rows of 4 are there for the product 3 × 4?

Multiplication is repeated addition.

$1 \times 4 = 4$
$2 \times 4 = 4 + 4$
$3 \times 4 = 4 + 4 + 4$

2. There are 16 students in a class. 4 students can sit at each table. How many tables are needed to fit all of the students?

| 3 | 4 | 5 | 6 |

Strategy: Model a division problem.

You can make a model to solve. Divide 16 students into 4 equal groups.

Practice On Your Own

Directions

Listen as your teacher reads each problem.
Choose the correct answer.

3. Which picture shows how three students should share eighteen crayons equally?

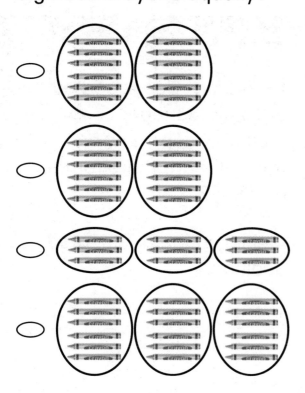

4. Maria has these balloons. She will give two balloons to each of her 7 friends. How many balloons will be left for Maria?

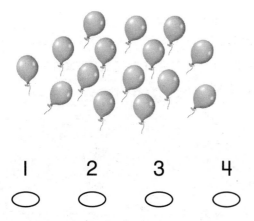

   1   2   3   4
  ○   ○   ○   ○

5. Erin earns $5 for every 2 dogs that she walks. How much will she earn for walking 10 dogs?

Erin's Dog Walking	
Dogs Walked	Earnings
2	$5
4	$10
6	$15
8	$20
10	

  $22 $25 $30 $35
  ○   ○   ○   ○

6. There are nine puppies at the park. Each puppy has four paws. How many puppy paws are there altogether?

  36   35   32   30
  ○   ○   ○   ○

Name _____

Practice by Standard: Number Sense

Standard Set 4.0: Students understand that fractions and decimals may refer to parts of a set and parts of a whole.

Directions

Listen as your teacher reads each problem.
Choose the correct answer.

QUICK Practice	QUICK Review

1. What fractional part of this figure is shaded?

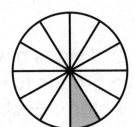

$\frac{1}{8}$ ⚬ $\frac{1}{9}$ ⚬ $\frac{1}{10}$ ⚬ $\frac{1}{12}$ ⚬

Strategy: Count the number of shaded parts. Compare this to the number of total parts.

The circle is divided into equal parts. How many equal parts do you see? How many of the equal parts are shaded? Use this information to write the fraction.

$$\frac{\text{number of shaded parts}}{\text{total number of parts}}$$

2. What fraction of the circles is shaded?

$\frac{1}{5}$ ⚬ $\frac{2}{5}$ ⚬ $\frac{3}{5}$ ⚬ $\frac{3}{8}$ ⚬

Strategy: Count the number of shaded circles. Compare this to the total number of circles.

How many circles are there in all?

How many of them are shaded?

Practice On Your Own

Directions
Listen as your teacher reads each problem.
Choose the correct answer.

3. Which fraction is equal to one whole?

$\frac{1}{7}$ $\frac{3}{4}$ $\frac{7}{7}$ $\frac{3}{8}$

○   ○   ○   ○

4. Which of the following fractions is the greatest?

$\frac{1}{5}$ $\frac{1}{2}$ $\frac{1}{12}$ $\frac{1}{8}$

○   ○   ○   ○

5. Look at the fraction bars. Which fraction bar shows one-fifth shaded?

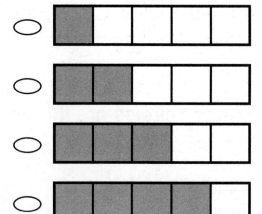

6. Nathan's family has five pets. Two of the pets are cats. What fraction of the family pets are cats?

$\frac{4}{5}$ $\frac{3}{5}$ $\frac{2}{5}$ $\frac{1}{5}$

○   ○   ○   ○

7. A teacher divides a whole class into groups to work in the class store. Each group has one-eighth of all the children in the class. How many groups are there?

2   4   6   8

○   ○   ○   ○

8. What fraction of the students on the playground are boys?

boy	boy	girl	girl	girl
boy	girl	girl	girl	girl

$\frac{1}{10}$ $\frac{3}{10}$ $\frac{6}{10}$ $\frac{7}{10}$

○   ○   ○   ○

Name _____

Practice by Standard: Number Sense

Standard Set 5.0: Students model and solve problems by representing, adding, and subtracting amounts of money.

Directions
Listen as your teacher reads each problem.
Choose the correct answer.

QUICK Practice	QUICK Review

I. Alicia has two quarters, four dimes, and three nickels. How much money does she have?

$0.85 ⬭ $1.05 ⬭

$1.15 ⬭ $1.30 ⬭

Strategy: Add values of coins to find the total amount of money. Start with the coin that has the greater value.

A quarter is worth $0.25 or 25¢. A dime is worth $0.10 or 10¢. A nickel is worth $0.05 or 5¢.

Think:
25¢ + 25¢ + 10¢ + 10¢ + 10¢ + 10¢ + 5¢ + 5¢ + 5¢

2. What is another way to write thirty-five cents?

35¢

$35.00 ⬭ $3.50 ⬭

$3.05 ⬭ $0.35 ⬭

Strategy: Use the decimal point and dollar sign to show amounts of money.

Write the dollars in between the dollar sign and the decimal point.

$2.25

dollars   cents

Practice On Your Own

Directions

Listen as your teacher reads each problem.
Choose the correct answer.

3. Evan has the money you see in the box. Which is a greater amount of money than Evan's?

⬭

⬭

⬭

⬭

4. Joy has one quarter, two dimes, and five nickels. How much money does she have?

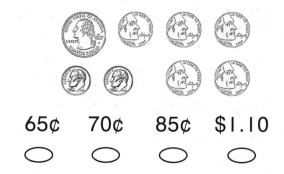

65¢   70¢   85¢ $1.10

◯   ◯   ◯   ◯

5. Hakeem has the money you see in the box.

If he buys a fruit smoothie for $2.00, how much money will he have left?

57¢   85¢ $1.20 $5.20

◯   ◯   ◯   ◯

Name _____

Practice by Standard: Number Sense

Standard Set 6.0: Students use estimation strategies in computation and problem solving that involve numbers that use the ones, tens, hundreds, and thousands places.

Directions

Listen as your teacher reads each problem.
Choose the correct answer.

QUICK Practice	QUICK Review
1. About how long is your math book? ◯ about 1 inch ◯ about 10 inches ◯ about 2 feet ◯ about 100 feet	**Strategy:** Choose the best unit. Then think how many of those units make up the object. Is a foot the unit you would use to measure the length of your math book? You can get rid of answers that do not make sense.
2. About how much sleep do you get in one week? ◯ about 30 minutes ◯ about 10 hours ◯ about 70 hours ◯ about 240 hours	**Strategy:** Use what you know about time to make a reasonable estimate. Estimate the amount of sleep you get in one night. Then think about the number of nights in one week. Use repeated addition to solve.

Practice On Your Own

Directions
Listen as your teacher reads each problem.
Choose the correct answer.

3. Sam makes $10 each day. He wants to know how much he will earn in 1 month. What is a reasonable estimate?

$200 ○ $400 ○

$300 ○ $700 ○

4. About how tall is a trash can?

5 inches ○   5 yards ○

3 feet ○   14 yards ○

5. Kimi is writing a story. She writes 62 pages the first month. If she keeps up this pace, about how many pages will she write in 4 months?

200 pages ○   280 pages ○

240 pages ○   300 pages ○

6. It takes Kendra about one half hour to complete a math worksheet. Tonight, Kendra completes 3 math worksheets. Estimate how many minutes Kendra was working.

30 minutes ○   90 minutes ○

60 minutes ○   2 hours ○

7. About how tall is the jungle gym on the playground?

5 inches ○   8 feet ○

45 inches ○   80 feet ○

8. Jamil earns $960 the first week. He earns $1,000 the second week. About how much money will he have after four weeks?

$500 ○ $3,000 ○

$2,000 ○ $4,000 ○

Name _____

Practice by Standard: Algebra and Functions

Standard Set 1.0: Students model, represent, and interpret number relationships to create and solve problems involving addition and subtraction.

Directions
Listen as your teacher reads each problem.
Choose the correct answer.

QUICK **Practice**	QUICK **Review**

1. What number goes in the box to make this number sentence true?

$$21 + \square = 11 + 21$$

  8   9   10   11
  ○   ○   ○   ○

Strategy: Choose the number that will give the same sum on both sides of the equals sign.

Remember that $2 + 5 = 5 + 2$. It does not matter what order you add whole numbers.

---

2. Carrie had eleven stuffed animals. She won some more at the fair. Now she has sixteen stuffed animals. Which number sentence could be used to show how many stuffed animals she won?

  ○ $11 + 16 = \square$

  ○ $11 + \square = 16$

  ○ $\square - 16 = 11$

  ○ $\square - 11 = 16$

Strategy: Let $\square$ be the number of stuffed animals Carrie won.

Carrie had eleven stuffed animals. She added $\square$ stuffed animals to this number and now she has 16.

How would you write a number sentence to find the missing number?

Practice On Your Own

Directions

Listen as your teacher reads each problem.
Choose the correct answer.

3. Look at the graph. Which number sentence shows how many hot dogs Rosa and Tat ate altogether?

Hot Dogs Eaten				
Rosa	🌭	🌭		
Tat	🌭	🌭	🌭	
Jack	🌭			

Key: 🌭 = 1

2 + 1 = 3 ⬭	2 + 3 = 5 ⬭
3 + 3 = 6 ⬭	12 − 6 = 12 ⬭

4. Paula jumped rope two hundred sixty-five times in a row. Omar jumped rope one hundred ninety-three times in a row. Which number sentence can be used to find how many more times Paula jumped rope in a row than Omar?

265
193

265 + 193 = ⬭	193 + 265 = ⬭
265 − 193 = ⬭	193 − 265 = ⬭

5. Look at the addition problem in the box. Which other problem has the same answer?

2 + 3 + 5 = 10

⬭ 3 + 5 + 10 = ☐
⬭ 3 + 4 + 5 = ☐
⬭ 5 + 10 + 2 = ☐
⬭ 3 + 5 + 2 = ☐

6. What number goes in the box to make this number sentence true?

6 + 9 = ☐ + 6

15	11	9	6
⬭	⬭	⬭	⬭

7. Look at the number sentence in the box. Which of the following has the same value as eight plus seven?

8 + 7 = 15

7 + 8 = ☐ ⬭	15 − 7 = ☐ ⬭
8 − 7 = ☐ ⬭	7 + 15 = ☐ ⬭

Name _____

Practice by Standard: Measurement and Geometry

Standard Set 1.0: Students understand that measurement is accomplished by identifying a unit of measure, iterating (repeating) that unit, and comparing it to the item to be measured.

Directions
Listen as your teacher reads each problem.
Choose the correct answer.

QUICK Practice

1. Jon's volleyball practice began at four o'clock P.M. and lasted two hours. At what time did practice end?

   2:00 A.M.   5:30 A.M.
   ⬭   ⬭

   5:00 P.M.   6:00 P.M.
   ⬭   ⬭

2. Look at the picture of the sea shell. Measure the length in inches. How long is the sea shell?

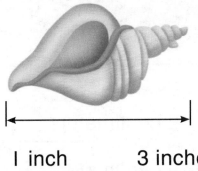

   1 inch   3 inches
   ⬭   ⬭

   2 inches   4 inches
   ⬭   ⬭

QUICK Review

Strategy: Add the amount of time at practice to the starting time. This will give you the ending time.

Add two hours to the starting time of 4:00 P.M. to find what time practice ended.

Strategy: Use an inch ruler to find the length of the shell.

Place one end of the shell at the 0 mark on the ruler.

Count the number of inches to the other end of the shell.

Practice On Your Own

Directions

Listen as your teacher reads each problem.
Choose the correct answer.

3. This pencil is about nine buttons long. About how many erasers long is the pencil?

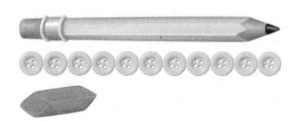

6   5   3   2
○   ○   ○   ○

4. LaToya did jumping jacks for one minute. How many seconds did she spend doing jumping jacks?

7   30   52   60
○   ○   ○   ○

5. Carmen will be going to a summer camp for 2 weeks. How many days will she be at summer camp?

60   52   30   14
○   ○   ○   ○

6. Look at the picture of the cup below. How many units tall is the cup?

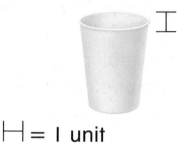

⊢ = 1 unit

6   5   4   3
○   ○   ○   ○

7. Look at the picture of the eraser. Measure the length of the eraser in centimeters. What is this length?

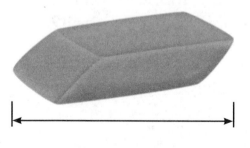

○   4 centimeters

○   5 centimeters

○   6 centimeters

○   7 centimeters

Name _____

Practice by Standard: Measurement and Geometry

Standard Set 2.0: Students identify and describe the attributes of common figures in the plane and of common objects in space.

Directions

Listen as your teacher reads each problem.
Choose the correct answer.

QUICK Practice	QUICK Review

1. How many edges does a rectangular prism have?

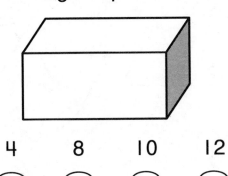

4	8	10	12
⭕	⭕	⭕	⭕

Strategy: An *edge* is a line segment where two faces meet.

Count the edges of the prism. Remember to count the ones that you cannot see.

---

2. Look at the pairs of shapes. Which is a pair of triangles?

⭕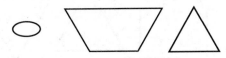

⭕

⭕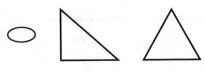

⭕

Strategy: A *triangle* is a shape that has three sides.

Think about triangles.

You know that triangles have 3 sides.

Look for the answer choice where both shapes have 3 sides.

Copyright © Macmillan/McGraw-Hill, a division of The McGraw-Hill Companies, Inc.

Practice On Your Own

Directions
Listen as your teacher reads each problem.
Choose the correct answer.

3. Which of the following shapes can be made from the two triangles?

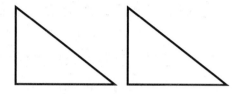

○

○

○

○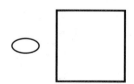

4. How many faces does a cube have?

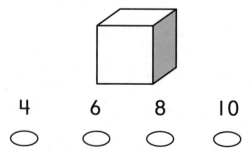

   4   6   8   10
   ○   ○   ○   ○

5. Look at the shape below. Which set of shapes could be used to form this shape?

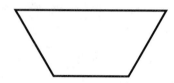

○

○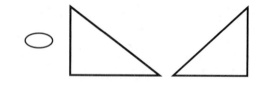

○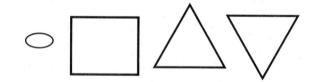

○

Name _____

Practice by Standard: Statistics, Data Analysis, and Probability

Standard Set 1.0: Students collect numerical data and record, organize, display, and interpret the data on bar graphs and other representations.

Directions
Listen as your teacher reads each problem.
Choose the correct answer.

QUICK Practice

1. What is the difference between the tallest height and the shortest height?

Student Heights	
Student	Height (in inches)
Conner	36
Yoko	48
Julio	45

○ 10 inches   ○ 12 inches

○ 11 inches   ○ 13 inches

2. Use the table of heights in Exercise 1. How much taller is Julio than Conner?

○ 2 inches   ○ 8 inches

○ 6 inches   ○ 9 inches

QUICK Review

Strategy: Look at the table. It shows student heights.

Find the tallest student.

Find the shortest student.

Subtract to find the difference.

Strategy: Find Julio's height. Find Conner's height.

Subtract to find how much taller Julio is than Conner.

Practice On Your Own

Directions

Listen as your teacher reads each problem.
Choose the correct answer.

3. The students in Mr. Alvarez's gym class are voting on their favorite activity. Nine students vote for basketball. Seven students vote for kick ball. Eleven students vote for soccer. Which tally chart shows these results?

Favorite Activity	
Basketball	ЖНТ II
Kick Ball	ЖНТ IIII
Soccer	ЖНТ ЖНТ I

○

Favorite Activity	
Basketball	ЖНТ ЖНТ I
Kick Ball	ЖНТ II
Soccer	ЖНТ IIII

○

Favorite Activity	
Basketball	ЖНТ III
Kick Ball	ЖНТ III
Soccer	ЖНТ ЖНТ I

○

Favorite Activity	
Basketball	ЖНТ IIII
Kick Ball	ЖНТ II
Soccer	ЖНТ ЖНТ I

○

4. Which graph matches the tally marks in the chart?

Favorite Pets	
Dog	ЖНТ III
Cat	ЖНТ
Fish	ЖНТ II

○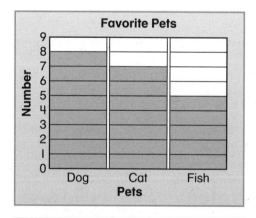

○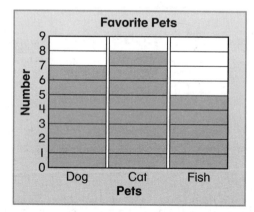

○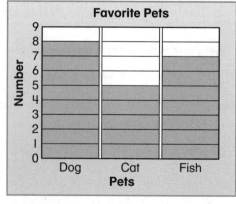

○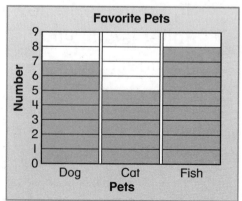

California Standards Review

Name _____

Practice by Standard: Statistics, Data Analysis, and Probability

Standard Set 2.0: Students demonstrate an understanding of patterns and how patterns grow and describe them in general ways.

Directions

Listen as your teacher reads each problem.
Choose the correct answer.

QUICK Practice

1. Look at the table. Which rule tells how to find the number of tires needed for eight bicycles?

Bicycle Tires Needed	
Number of Bicycles	Number of Tires
1	2
2	4
3	6

- ⬭ multiply 8 by 2
- ⬭ divide 8 by 2
- ⬭ add 2 and 8
- ⬭ subtract 2 from 8

2. Look at the pattern below. What is the next number?

1, 3, 5, 7, 9, 11, 13, ☐

14   15   16   17
⬭   ⬭   ⬭   ⬭

QUICK Review

Strategy: Look for a pattern in the table.

Two tires are needed for each bicycle.

You can multiply the number of bicycles by 2 to find the number of tires needed.

You can also use repeated addition to find the number of tires needed.

Strategy: Look for a pattern in the set of numbers.

The pattern is adding two each time.

You can find the next number by adding 2 to 13.

Practice On Your Own

Directions

Listen as your teacher reads each problem.
Choose the correct answer.

3. The table shows the number of children with each adult on a field trip. If there are thirty children, how many adults are there?

Field Trip	
Adults	Children
1	5
2	10
3	15
4	20

9   8   7   6

○   ○   ○   ○

4. Look at the pattern below. What is the missing number?

4, 8, ☐, 16, 20, 24

9   10   12   18

○   ○   ○   ○

5. Look at the pattern below. Which rule tells how to find the next number in the pattern?

1, 4, 7, 10, 13, 16

○ add 3   ○ subtract 2

○ add 4   ○ multiply by 3

6. Selam and Angie are playing a game. Each time a player lands on a bonus space, the player earns ten points. How many points would be earned if a player lands on six bonus spaces?

Bonus Spaces	Points Earned
1	10
2	20
3	30

50   60   70   80

○   ○   ○   ○

7. Ling has a collection of dimes. Each dime is worth ten cents. How many dimes does Ling have if they are worth one hundred forty cents altogether?

Coin Collection	
Number of Dimes	Value of Coins
1	10¢
2	20¢
3	30¢
4	40¢

28   25   14   12

○   ○   ○   ○

Name _____

Practice by Standard: Mathematical Reasoning

Standard Set 1.0: Students make decisions about how to set up a problem.

Directions
Listen as your teacher reads each problem.
Choose the correct answer.

QUICK Practice	QUICK Review
1. James placed a forty-foot long rope on the field. He put one cone at the beginning and one at the end of the rope. Then he put another cone every ten feet in between along the rope. Which drawing below could be used to find how many cones are needed in all?	**Strategy:** Use a drawing to help you solve the problem. Which drawing shows a cone at the beginning, a cone at the end, and a cone every ten feet for forty feet?

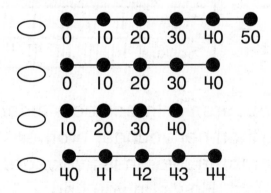

QUICK Practice	QUICK Review

2. In Exercise 1, how many cones are needed for the forty-foot length?
 	
   4   5   6   7
  ◯   ◯   ◯   ◯
	Strategy: Use the drawing to help you solve the problem.
	
	Count the cones in the drawing.

Practice On Your Own

Directions
Listen as your teacher reads each problem.
Choose the correct answer.

3. Ron is using square tiles to make squares of different sizes. The drawings below show the first two sizes. Which drawing will help you find the next size?

I square tile   4 square tiles

4. Mandy has a collection of quarters. She makes a pattern to show how many cents she has in quarters. Which pattern can she use to show the value of her quarters?

- ○ 1, 2, 3, 4, 5
- ○ 5, 10, 15, 20, 25
- ○ 10, 20, 30, 40, 50
- ○ 25, 50, 75, 100, 125

5. Taye has three stickers for every two stickers Sonia has. Taye has fifteen stickers in all. Which chart will help you find how many stickers Sonia has?

6. Lauren is three years older than her younger brother Martin. Martin is five years old. How can you find Lauren's age?

- ○ subtract 3 from 5
- ○ add 3 to 5
- ○ multiply 3 and 5
- ○ divide 5 by 3

Practice by Standard: Mathematical Reasoning

Standard Set 2.0: Students solve problems and justify their reasoning.

Directions
Listen as your teacher reads each problem.
Choose the correct answer.

QUICK Practice

1. Eduardo's garden has twelve flowers. All the flowers are roses or tulips. There are twice as many roses as tulips. How many roses are there?

   4   6   8   9
   ⬭   ⬭   ⬭   ⬭

2. Amna has a one dollar bill, one quarter, and two nickels. She says she has $1.35. Which number sentence could be used to check Amna's statement?

   ⬭ $1 + $0.25 + $0.25 + $0.05

   ⬭ $1 + $0.25 + $0.05 + $0.05

   ⬭ $1.35 − $1.00 − $0.25 − $0.05

   ⬭ $1 + $0.25 + $0.50 + $0.50

QUICK Review

Strategy: Guess and check to find the number of roses.

Guess different numbers of roses and tulips. The sum of the numbers must be twelve.

Tulips	Roses
2	10
3	9
4	8

Strategy: Add the values of the dollar bill and the coins to find the total amount of money.

A quarter is worth $0.25.

Practice On Your Own

Directions

Listen as your teacher reads each problem.
Choose the correct answer.

3. The second graders collected 45 canned goods during the first day of a food drive. They collected 61 canned goods on the second day. How many cans are there in all?

- ○ There are 16 cans.
  $61 - 45 = 16$
- ○ There are 106 cans.
  $61 \times 45 = 106$
- ○ There are 96 cans.
  $61 + 45 = 96$
- ○ There are 106 cans.
  $61 + 45 = 106$

4. Mickey scored two times as many points as Keisha. Mickey scored six points in all. How many points did Keisha score?

- ○ Keisha scored 12 points.
  $6 \times 2 = 12$
- ○ Keisha scored 2 points.
  $6 \div 3 = 2$
- ○ Keisha scored 4 points.
  $6 - 2 = 4$
- ○ Keisha scored 3 points.
  $6 \div 2 = 3$

5. Look at the pattern below. What is the missing number in the pattern?

5, 10, 15, ☐ 25, 30

- ○ 16–skip count by 1s
- ○ 16–skip count by 5s
- ○ 18–skip count by 3s
- ○ 20–skip count by 5s

6. Three students are standing in line. Roberto is in front of Olivia. Lindsay is behind Olivia. You say Lindsay is last in line. Which answer could be used to check this?

- ○ Roberto Lindsay Olivia
- ○ Lindsay Olivia Roberto
- ○ Roberto Olivia Lindsay
- ○ Olivia Roberto Lindsay

Name _____

Practice by Standard: Mathematical Reasoning

Standard Set 3.0: Students note connections between one problem and another.

Directions
Listen as your teacher reads each problem.
Choose the correct answer.

QUICK Practice

1. One of these shapes does not belong. Choose which shape does not belong and why.

   ○ ▯ It has 6 faces.

   ○ ▱ It has 12 edges.

   ○ ▯ It is a plane shape.

   ○ ▱ It has 8 vertices.

QUICK Review

Strategy: Note differences and similarities between plane shapes and solid shapes.

List the attributes of each shape to decide which shape is different.

▯	▯	▱
• rectangular prism • solid shape • 6 faces • 8 vertices • 12 edges	• rectangle • plane shape • 4 sides • 4 vertices	• rectangular prism • solid shape • 6 faces • 8 vertices • 12 edges

2. Look at the number patterns. What do they have in common?

   Pattern 1: $5, $10, $15

   Pattern 2: 90, 85, 80, 75

   ○ counting by 5s

   ○ repeating patterns

   ○ patterns are growing

   ○ involve money

Strategy: Find a connection between two patterns.

Test each answer choice and decide which statements are true and which statements are false. The statement that is true for both patterns is the answer.

Practice On Your Own

Directions
Listen as your teacher reads each problem.
Choose the correct answer.

3. How are these shapes related?

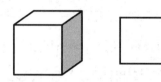

○ Both have 4 vertices.

○ Both are 2-dimensional.

○ A cube has square faces.

○ A square is the same as a cube.

4. What is the connection between these two number patterns?

Pattern I: 32, 28, 24, 20...

Pattern 2: 10, 8, 6, 4...

○ counting by 2s

○ getting bigger

○ getting smaller

○ counting by 4s

5. What do these number sentences have in common?

$$3 + 4 = 7$$
$$7 - 4 = 3$$

○ They both equal zero.

○ They both find a sum.

○ They represent fractions.

○ They are part of the same fact family.

6. What do these number sentences have in common?

$$5 + 5 + 5 = 15$$
$$3 \times 5 = 15$$

○ They both equal 15.

○ They both find a product.

○ They belong to the same fact family.

○ They both find a sum.

Looking Ahead

to the Grade 3 Standards

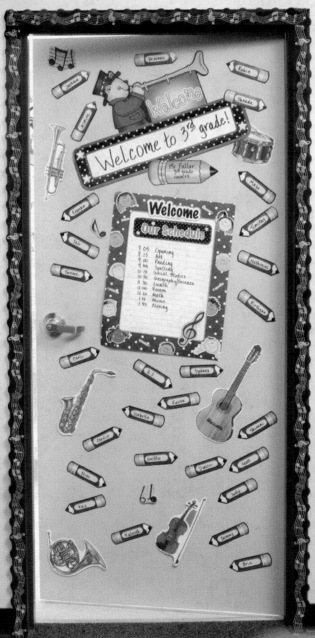

Let's Look Ahead

Name _____

Explore Probability

Get Ready

Main Idea

I will identify events as certain, likely, or unlikely.

Vocabulary

certain

likely

unlikely

You can tell if an event is certain, likely, or unlikely.

Certain	Likely	Unlikely
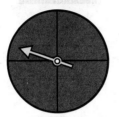	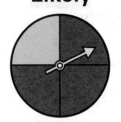	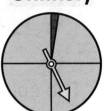
Landing on red is certain. It will always happen.	Landing on red is likely. It will probably happen.	Landing on red is unlikely. It will probably never happen.

✓ Check

Look at each spinner to answer the question.
Circle the answer.

1. The spinner landing on red is

   certain
   likely
   unlikely

2. The spinner landing on green is

   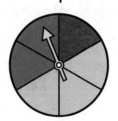
   certain
   likely
   unlikely

3. The spinner landing on blue is

   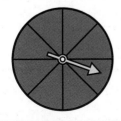
   certain
   likely
   unlikely

4. The spinner landing on purple is

   certain
   likely
   unlikely

5. **Talk About It** What does certain mean? What does unlikely mean?

▶ **Practice**

Look at each spinner to answer the question.
Circle the answer.

6. The spinner landing on green is

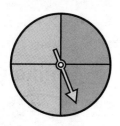

certain

likely

unlikely

7. The spinner landing on blue is

certain

likely

unlikely

8. The spinner landing on green is

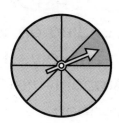

certain

likely

unlikely

9. The spinner landing on yellow is

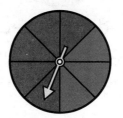

certain

likely

unlikely

Problem Solving

10. Reasoning Mr. Franklin's students pick a color and spin the wheel. If it lands on the color they picked, they get a prize. Here are the colors each of his students picked.

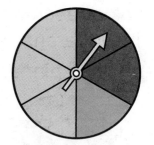

Mary – blue   Rico – yellow
Seth – green   Marita – red

Which student is most likely to win a prize? _____

Which student will never win a prize? _____

Explain why. _____

_____

_____

Math at Home Activity: Lay out 10 pennies and 2 dimes.
Ask your child which coin is most likely to be picked up.

Name _____

 ## 2 Likely and Unlikely Events

Get Ready

Main Idea

I will identify events as likely or unlikely to happen.

Review Vocabulary

likely

unlikely

Sometimes you can tell if an event is **likely** or **unlikely** to happen.

How likely is it that James will get a ◄█████████████► instead of a ◄████████►?

There are more ◄█████████████► than ◄████████►. James is more likely to pick a ◄█████████████►.

James picks a crayon out of a bag. He records the color on the tally chart. Then he puts the crayon back in the bag. James does this 10 times.

Color Chosen	
Color	Tally
red	⊮⊮ ‖
green	‖‖

Check

Tell if the event is likely or unlikely to happen. Then follow the steps 10 times to complete the tally chart.

1. 4 🔲 and 2 ⬛ are in a bag. You are _____ to pick 🔲 instead of ⬛. Circle.

   likely   unlikely

2. Place 4 🔲 and 2 ⬛ in a bag.

Color Chosen	
Color	Tally
green	
purple	

3. **Talk About It** Do your results from your tally chart match your answer in Exercise 1? Explain.

Tell how likely it is that the event will happen.
Then follow the steps 10 times to complete
the tally chart.

1. Pick a cube.
2. Record the color
   in the tally chart.
3. Return the cube
   to the bag.

4. 2 ■ and 6 ▢ are in a bag.
   You are _____ to pick ■
   instead of ▢. Circle.

   likely   unlikely

5. Place 2 ■ and 4 ▢ in a bag.

Color Chosen	
Color	Tally
red	
yellow	

6. 5 ▢ and 4 ▢ are in a bag.
   You are _____ to pick a
   ▢ instead of a ▢. Circle.

   likely   unlikely

7. Place 5 ▢ and 4 ▢ in a bag.

Color Chosen	
Color	Tally
orange	
yellow	

Problem Solving

8. **Reasoning** Terry put 5 ■ and 5 ▢ in a bag.
   Would Terry be more likely to pick a ■ or a ▢?

   Explain. _____

   _____

   _____

   _____

Math at Home Activity: Have your child put 2 red pens and 4 blue pens
in a shopping bag. Ask your child which one is likely to be picked first.

Name _____

 Cups And Gallons

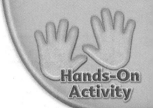

Get Ready

Main Idea

I will estimate and measure liquid volume.

Vocabulary

cup

gallon

You can use **cups** and **gallons** to measure how much a container can hold.

CUP

GALLON

 **Check**

Circle the better estimate.

Container	Estimate
1.	about 2 cups about 10 cups
2.	about 3 gallons about 30 gallons
3.	about 1 cup about 1 gallon

4. **Talk About It** Which unit of measure, cups or gallons, would be best to use to find out how much a water bottle can hold? Why?

Looking Ahead   Lesson 3   four hundred seventy-one   **471**

Find the container. Circle the better estimate.
Measure. Circle the closer measure.

Find the container.	Circle the estimate.	Circle the measure.
5.	about 2 gallons about 10 gallons	2 gallons 10 gallons
6.	about 1 gallon about 2 gallons	1 gallon 2 gallon
7.	about 1 cup about 6 cups	1 cup 6 cups
8.	about 10 cups about 2 cups	10 cups 2 cups
9.	about 1 cup about 3 cups	1 cup 3 cups

10. WRITING IN ▶MATH Explain how you could find how many cups in a gallon.

_____

_____

_____

Math at Home Activity: Use a cup measure. Ask your child to estimate how many cups it would take to fill different containers. Then have your child measure.

Name _____

 # Milliliters and Liters

Get Ready

Main Idea

I will estimate and measure capacity using milliliters and liters.

Vocabulary

milliliter

liter

You can use **liters** and **milliliters** to measure how much a container can hold.

This bottle can hold 1 liter.

This dropper can hold 1 milliliter of water.

Check

Circle the better estimate.

Container	Estimate
1.	about 1 milliliter about 1 liter
2.	about 1 milliliter about 1 liter
3.	about 1 milliliter about 1 liter

4. **Talk About It** Does a bathroom sink hold more or less than 1 liter? How do you know?

Find the container. Circle the better estimate.
Measure. Circle the closer measure.

Find the container.	Circle the estimate.	Circle the measure.
5.	about I milliliter about I liter	I liter I milliliter
6.	about I milliliter about I liter	I liter I milliliter
7.	about I milliliter about I liter	I liter I milliliter
8.	about I milliliter about I liter	I liter I milliliter

H.O.T. Problem

9. Melissa filled 6 glasses with I liter of juice.
   How many glasses could she fill with 3 liters
   of juice?

   _____ + _____ + _____ = _____ glasses

   Explain how you solved.

   _____

   _____

   _____

Math at Home Activity: Have your child find and show you a
container that holds more than 1 liter and a container that holds
less than 1 liter.

Name _____

 # Ounces and Pounds

Get Ready

Main Idea

I will estimate and measure weight using ounces and pounds.

Vocabulary

ounce

pound

You can measure weight in **ounces** and **pounds**.

16 ounces = 1 pound

A slice of bread weighs about 1 ounce.	A loaf of bread weighs about 1 pound.
slice	loaf

1 ounce	1 pound

Check

Circle the better estimate.

Find the item.	Circle the estimate.
1. 	about 1 pound about 1 ounce
2.	about 1 pound about 1 ounce
3.	about 1 pound about 1 ounce

4. **Talk About It** Which weighs more, 16 ounces of bricks or 1 pound of markers? Why?

Practice

Find the item. Circle the better estimate. Then measure.
Circle the closer measure.

Find the item.	Circle the estimate.	Circle the measure.
5.	about 1 pound about 1 ounce	1 pound 1 ounce
6.	about 1 pound about 1 ounce	1 pound 1 ounce
7.	about 1 pound about 1 ounce	1 pound 1 ounce
8.	about 1 pound about 1 ounce	1 pound 1 ounce
9.	1 pound 1 ounce	1 pound 1 ounce

H.O.T. Problem

10. **Explaining Math** If you have a 1-pound bag of flour on one side of a balance scale and a 12-ounce can on the other side, what will happen to the scale? Explain why.

_____

_____

_____

_____

Math at Home Activity: Collect four items from around the house. Ask your child to put them in order by weight.

Name _____

6 Grams and Kilograms

Get Ready

Main Idea

I will estimate and measure mass in grams and kilograms.

Vocabulary

gram

kilogram

You can measure mass in **grams** and **kilograms**.

1,000 grams = 1 kilogram

One piece of dog food is about 1 gram.

1 gram

A can of dog food is about 1 kilogram.

1 kilogram

Check

Circle the better estimate.

Item	Circle the estimate.
1. 	about 1 gram about 5 grams
2.	about 2 grams about 10 grams
3.	about 1 kilogram about 4 kilograms

4. **Talk About It** Is a large object always heavier than a smaller object? Explain.

Find the item. Circle the better estimate. Then
measure. Circle the closer measure.

Find the item.	Circle the estimate.	Circle the measure.
5.	about 3 grams about 15 grams	3 grams 15 grams
6.	about 10 grams about 1 gram	10 grams 1 gram
7.	about 5 kilograms about 15 kilograms	5 kilograms 15 kilograms
8.	about 35 kilograms about 10 kilograms	35 kilograms 10 kilograms
9.	about 1000 grams about 100 grams	1000 grams 100 grams

H.O.T. Problem

10. **Explaining Math** If a can of soup is 330 grams,
    how many cans of soup would be about
    1 kilogram?

    about _____ cans of soup

    Explain why. _____

_____

478   four hundred seventy-eight

Math at Home Activity: While at the grocery store, ask your
child to find items that show the mass in kilograms and/or grams.

Student Handbook

Built-In Workbook

How to Use the Student Handbook

Use the Student Handbook

- when you need more practice with addition facts and subtraction facts

- when you need to show different ways to make numbers, show the order of numbers, count on to add, count back to subtract, or write numbers as hundreds, tens, and ones

- when you need to know the meaning of a math word

- when you need to find number patterns, to order numbers, or to skip count

- when you need help writing the number names

- when you need help measuring inches, centimeters, feet, and yards

Glossary/Glosario

English A Español

add (addition) Join together sets to find the total or sum. The opposite of *subtract*. (page 53)

$$2 + 5 = 7$$

suma (adición) Unir conjuntos para calcular el total o la suma. Lo opuesto a la *resta*.

$$2 + 5 = 7$$

---

addend Any numbers or quantities being added together. (page 53)
In $2 + 3 = 5$, 2 is an addend and 3 is an addend.

$$2 + 3 = 5$$
↑ ↑

sumando Cualquier número o cantidad que se suma. $2 + 3 = 5$, 2 es un sumando y 3 es un sumando.

$$2 + 3 = 5$$
↑ ↑

---

addition sentence A math sentence that has an addition sign in it. (page 53)

$$4 + 5 = 9$$

expresión de suma Una expresión matemática que tiene un signo de suma.

$$4 + 5 = 9$$

---

after Follow in place or time. (page 31)

5 6 7 8

6 is just *after* 5

después Que sigue en lugar o en tiempo.

5 6 7 8

6 viene inmediatamente después del 5

---

analog clock A clock that has an **hour hand** and a **minute hand.** (page 393)

minute hand  hour hand

reloj analógico Reloj que tiene un horario y un minutero.

minutero  manecilla horaria

Glossary/Glosario

English		Español
	A	

array Objects displayed in rows and columns. (page 253)

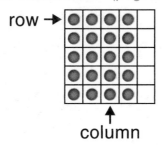

row →

↑
column

arreglo Objetos presentados en filas y columnas.

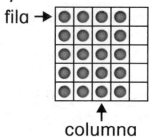

fila →

↑
columna

B

bar graph A graph that uses bars to show data. (page 123)

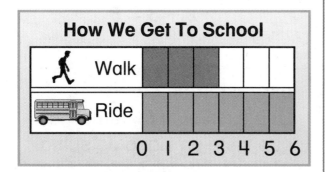

How We Get To School

Walk
Ride

0 1 2 3 4 5 6

gráfica de barras Gráfica que usa barras para mostrar datos.

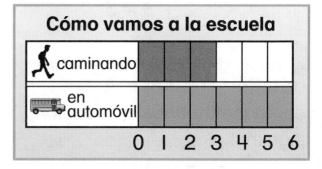

Cómo vamos a la escuela

caminando
en automóvil

0 1 2 3 4 5 6

before (page 31)

5 6 7 8

6 is just *before* 7

antes

5 6 7 8

6 viene inmediate mente antes del 7

between (page 31)

47 48 49 50

49 is *between* 48 and 50

entre

47 48 49 50

49 está entre 47 y 50

C

cent ¢ (page 211)

1¢ 1 cent

centavo ¢

1¢ 1 centavo

Glossary/Glosario

English	C	**Español**

centimeter (cm) A metric unit for measuring length. (page 387)

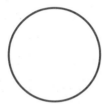

centimeters

centímetro (cm) Una unidad métrica de medida alturas.

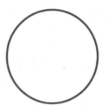

centímetros

---

circle A closed, round plane shape. (page 353)

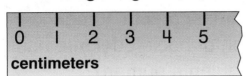

círculo Figura redonda y cerrada.

---

compare Look at objects, shapes, or numbers and see how they are alike or different.

(page 33)

comparar Observar objetos, formas o números y ver en qué se parecen o en qué se diferencian.

---

cone A solid shape that narrows to a point from a circular base.

(page 347)

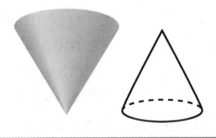

cono Figura sólida que se estrecha hasta formar un punto desde una base circular.

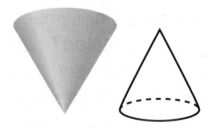

---

count back On a number line, start at the greater number (5) and count back (3). (page 83)

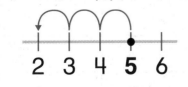

2 3 4 **5** 6

5 − 3 = 2   Count back 3.

contar al revés En una recta numérica, comienza en el número 5 y cuenta 3 al revés.

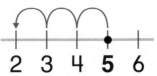

2 3 4 **5** 6

5 − 3 = 2   Cuenta 3 al revés.

Glossary/Glosario

English		Español

count on (or count up) Start at a number on a number line and count up to the next number. (page 55)

$$4 + 2 = 6$$

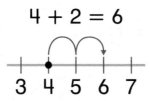

3 4 5 6 7

contar hacia adelante Comenzar en una recta numéricarecta numérica y contar hacia adelante hasta el siguiente número.

$$4 + 2 = 6$$

3 4 5 6 7

---

cube A solid shape with 6 square faces. (page 347)

cubo Figura tridimensional con 6 caras cuadradas.

---

cylinder A solid shape that looks like a can. (page 347)

cilindro Figura sólida con forma de lata.

---

data Numbers or symbols, sometimes collected from a survey or experiment, that show information. *Data* is plural.

(page 113)

Name	Number of Pets
Mary	3
James	1
Alonzo	4

datos Números o símbolos que, a veces, se recopilan mediante una encuesta o experimento, para mostrar información. *Datos* es un nombre plural.

Nombre	Número de mascotas
Maria	3
James	1
Alonzo	4

Glossary/Glosario

English	D	Español

decimal point A period used in a decimal number. (page 219)

$2.95.
↑

punto decimal Punto que se utiliza en un número decimal.

$2.95.
↑

---

difference The answer to a subtraction problem. (page 83)

$3 - 1 = 2$
↑

The difference is 2.

diferencia Resultado de un problema de sustracción.

$3 - 1 = 2$
↑

La diferencia es 2.

---

digit A symbol used to write numbers. The ten digits are 0, 1, 2, 3, 4, 5, 6, 7, 8, 9. (page 21)

dígito Símbolo que se utiliza para representar números. Los diez dígitos son 0, 1, 2, 3, 4, 5, 6, 7, 8, 9.

---

digital clock A clock that uses only numbers to show time. (page 393)

reloj digital Reloj que sólo utiliza números para mostrar la hora.

---

dime dime = 10¢ or 10 cents (page 211)

head   tail

moneda de 10 centavos moneda de 10 centavos = 10¢ ó 10 centavos

cara   escudo

---

divide (division) To separate into equal groups. (page 267)

$9 \div 3 = 3$

dividir (división) Separar en grupos iguales.

$9 \div 3 = 3$

Glossary/Glosario

English		Español
	D	

division sentence A math sentence that has a division sign in it. (page 269)

$$12 \div 3 = 4$$

enunciado de división Enunciado matemático que contiene un signo de división.

$$12 \div 3 = 4$$

---

dollar ($) one dollar =100¢ or 100 cents. Also written as $1.00. (page 219)

front

back

signo de dólar ($) un dólar = 100¢ ó 100 centavos

frente

dorso

---

doubles (and near doubles) Two addends that are the same number. (page 59)

$6 + 6 = 12 \leftarrow$ doubles
$6 + 7 = 13 \leftarrow$ near doubles

dobles (y casi dobles) Dos sumandos que son el mismo número.

$7 + 7 = 14 \leftarrow$ dobles
$7 + 8 = 15 \leftarrow$ casi dobles

	E	

edge The line where two sides or *faces* meet. (page 349)

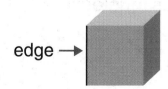

edge →

arista La línea donde se encuentran dos lados *o caras*.

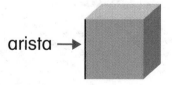

arista →

Glossary/Glosario

English		Español

equal groups Each group has the same number of objects. (page 249)

There are four equal groups of counters.

grupos iguales Cada grupo tiene el mismo número de objetos.

Hay cuatro grupos iguales de fichas.

---

equal parts Each part is the same size. (page 285)

This sandwich is cut into 2 equal parts.

partes iguales Cada parte es del mismo tamaño.

Este sándwich está cortado en 2 partes iguales.

---

estimate Find a number close to an exact amount. (page 27)

47 + 22 rounds to 50 + 20
The estimate is 70.

estimar Hallar un número cercano a la cantidad exacta.

47 + 22 se redondea a 50 + 20. La estimación es 70.

---

expanded form
The representation of a number as a sum that shows the value of each digit. Sometimes called *expanded notation*. (page 321)

536 is written as 500 + 30 + 6.

forma desarrollada La representación de un número como suma que muestra el valor de cada dígito. Algunas veces se llama *notación desarrollada*.

536 se escribe como 500 + 30 + 6.

Glossary/Glosario

English	**Español**
face The flat part of a 3-dimensional figure. (page 349)	**cara** La parte plana de una figura tridimensional.

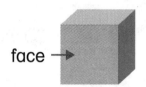

A square is a face of a cube.

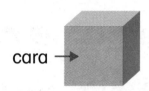

Un cuadrado es la cara de un cubo.

---

fact family Addition and subtraction sentences that use the same numbers. (page 99)

$6 + 7 = 13$ $13 - 7 = 6$
$7 + 6 = 13$ $13 - 6 = 7$

familia de operaciones Enunciados de adición y sustracción que utilizan los mismos números.

$6 + 7 = 13$ $13 - 7 = 6$
$7 + 6 = 13$ $13 - 6 = 7$

---

factor A number that is multiplied by another number. (page 257)

$$3 \times 6 = 18$$
↑   ↑

factor Número que se multiplica por otro número.

$$3 \times 6 = 18$$
↑   ↑

---

foot (ft) A unit to measure length. The plural is *feet*. (page 381)

1 foot = 12 inches

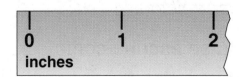

pie (p) Unidad para medir longitud. El plural es *pies*.

1 pie = 12 pulgadas

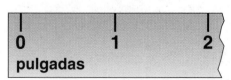

Glossary/Glosario

English		Español

fraction A number that represents part of a whole or part of a set. (page 285)

$$\left(\frac{1}{2}\right), \left(\frac{1}{3}\right), \left(\frac{1}{4}\right), \left(\frac{3}{4}\right)$$

fracción Número que representa la parte de un todo o la parte de un conjunto.

$$\left(\frac{1}{2}\right), \left(\frac{1}{3}\right), \left(\frac{1}{4}\right), \left(\frac{3}{4}\right)$$

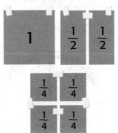

Fractions

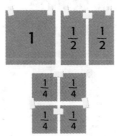

Fraccións

group A set of objects (page 299)

grupo Conjunto o grupo de elementos

group of 4

grupo de 4

half-dollar half-dollar = 50¢ or 50 cents (page 213)

medio dólar medio dólar = 50¢ ó 50 centavos

head   tail

cara   escudo

Glossary/Glosario

English		Español

hexagon A plane shape that has six sides. (page 353)

hexágono Figura que tiene seis lados.

---

hour A unit of time. (page 401)

1 hour = 60 minutes

hora Unidad de tiempo.

1 hora = 60 minutos

---

hour hand The shorter hand on a clock that tells the hour. (page 393)

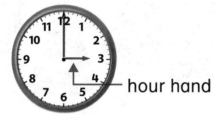
— hour hand

manecilla horaria La manecilla del reloj que indica la hora. Es la manecilla más corta.

— manecilla horaria

---

hundreds The numbers 100–999. (page 315)
In the number 234, the 2 is in the hundreds place.

centenas Los números del 100–999.
En el número 234, el 2 está en el lugar de las centenas.

---

inch (in.) A customary unit for measuring length. The plural is *inches.* (page 379)

12 inches = 1 foot

pulgada (pulg) Unidad inglesa para medir longitud. El plural es *pulgadas.*

12 pulgadas = 1 pie

Glossary/Glosario

English | Español

inverse operation Operations that undo each other. (page 93) Addition and subtraction are inverse or opposite operations.

operación inversa Operaciones que se anulan entre sí. La adición y la sustracción son operaciones inversas u opuestas.

is equal to = (page 33)

6 = 6

6 is equal to or the same as 6

es igual a =

6 = 6

6 es igual a o lo mismo que 6

is greater than > (page 33)

7 > 2

7 is greater than 2

es mayor que >

7 > 2

7 es mayor que 2

is less than < (page 33)

4 < 7

4 is less than 7

es menor que <

4 < 7

4 es menor que 7

Glossary/Glosario

English	K	**Español**

key Tells what (or how many) each symbol stands for. (page 115)

Favorite Pet			
Fish	☺	☺	☺
Dog	☺		
Cat	☺	☺	

Key: ☺ = 2 votes

clave Indica qué o cuánto representa cada símbolo.

Animal doméstico favorito			
Pez	☺	☺	☺
Perro	☺		
Gato	☺	☺	

Clave: ☺ = 2 votes

L

length How long or how far away something is. (page 377)

length

longitud La longitud de algo o a qué distancia está.

longitud

M

measure To find the length, height, or weight using standard or nonstandard units. (page 377)

medir Hallar la longitud, altura o el peso usando unidades estándar o no estándar.

---

meter (m) A metric unit for measuring length. A meter is about the length of a baseball bat or the width of a door. (page 389)

1 meter = 100 centimeters

metro (m) Unidad métrica para medir longitud. Es aproximadamente del largo de un bate de béisbol o del ancho de una puerta.

1 metro = 100 centímetros

Glossary/Glosario

English	M	Español

minute (min) A unit used to measure time. (page 401)

I minute = 60 seconds

minuto (min) Unidad que se usa para medir el tiempo.

I minuto = 60 segundos

---

minute hand The longer hand on a clock that tells the minutes. (page 393)

minute hand

minutero La manecilla más larga de un reloj que indica los minutos.

minutero

---

missing addend (page 97)

$$9 + \_\_\_\_ = 16$$

The missing addend is 7.

sumando desconocido

$$9 + \_\_\_\_ = 16$$

El sumando desconocido es 7.

---

mode The number(s) that occurs most often in a set of numbers. A set can have more than one mode. (page 133)

7, 4, 7, 10, 7, and 2
The *mode* is 7.

moda El número o los números que ocurren con más frecuencia en un conjunto de números. Un conjunto puede tener más de una moda.

7, 4, 7, 10, 7 y 2. La *moda* es 7.

Glossary/Glosario

English		Español

multiples A multiple of a number is the *product* of that number and any whole number. (page 253)

15 is a multiple of 5 because
$3 \times 5 = 15$.

múltiplos Un múltiplo de un número es el *producto* de ese número por cualquier número entero.

15 es un múltiplo de 5 porque
$3 \times 5 = 15$.

---

multiplication sentence
A math sentence that has a multiplication sign in it. (page 251)

$5 \times 4 = 20$

enunciado de multiplicación
Un enunciado matemático que contiene un signo de multiplicación.

$5 \times 4 = 20$

---

multiply (multiplication)
Find the product. The operation of repeated addition of the same number. (page 251)

$4 \times 2 = 8$
Four groups of two are equal to eight or
$2 + 2 + 2 + 2 = 8$.

multiplicar (multiplicación)
Calcular el producto. La operación de adición repetida del mismo número.

$4 \times 2 = 8$.
Cuatro grupos de dos son iguales a ocho ó
$2 + 2 + 2 + 2 = 8$.

---

nickel nickel = 5¢ or 5 cents
(page 211)

head   tail

moneda de cinco centavos moneda de cinco centavos = 5¢ ó 5 centavos

cara   escudo

Glossary/Glosario

English		Español

N

number line A line with number labels. (page 31)

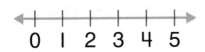

recta numéricarecta numérica Recta con rótulos de números.

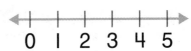

number sentence An expression using numbers and the = sign, or the < or > sign. (page 53)

$$5 + 4 = 9; 8 > 5$$

enunciado numérico Expresión que usa números y el signo = o los signos < o >.

$$5 + 4 = 9; 8 > 5$$

O

ones A place value of a number. (page 17)

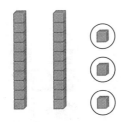

23

This number has 3 ones.

unidades El valor de posición de un número.

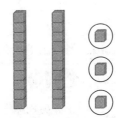

23

Este número tiene 3 unidades.

P

parallelogram A plane shape that has four sides. Each pair of opposite sides is equal and parallel. (page 353)

paralelogramo Figura que tiene cuatro lados. Cada par de lados opuestos es igual y paralelo.

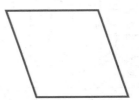

Glossary/Glosario

English	 P	Español

pattern An order that a set of objects or numbers follows over and over. (page 37)

A, A, B, A, A, B, A, A, B

patrón Orden que sigue una y otra vez un conjunto de objetos o números.

A, A, B, A, A, B, A, A, B

---

penny penny = 1¢ or 1 cent (page 211)

head   tail

moneda de un centavo Centavo = 1¢ ó 1 centavo

cara   escudo

---

pictograph A graph that uses the same picture or symbol to show the data. (page 115)

Vehicles In Our Parking Lot					
Trucks	◉	◉			
Cars	◉	◉	◉	◉	◉
Buses	◉	◉	◉		

Key: ◉ = 2

pictografía Gráfica que utiliza la misma imagen o símbolo para mostrar los datos.

Vehículos En Nuestro Estacionamiento					
Camiones	◉	◉			
Autos	◉	◉	◉	◉	◉
Autobuses	◉	◉	◉		

Clave: ◉ = 2

---

picture graph A graph that has different pictures to show information collected. (page 115)

How I Get to School								
Bus								
Bike								
Walk								

gráfica de imagen Gráfica que tiene diferentes imágenes para mostrar la información recopilada.

Cómo Voy a la Escuela							
Autobús							
Bicicleta							
Caminando							

Glossary/Glosario

English	P	Español
place value The value given to a *digit* by its place in a number. (page 21)		**valor de posición** El valor dado a un *dígito* según su posición en un número.
365 3 is in the hundreds place 6 is in the tens place 5 is in the ones place		365 3 está en el lugar de las centenas 6 está en el lugar de las decenas 5 está en el lugar de las unidades
plane shape A figure such as a triangle or square that is flat or 2-dimensional. (page 353)		**figura plana** Figura como un triángulo o un cuadrado que es plana (o bidimensional).
product The answer to a multiplication problem. (page 253) $3 \times 4 = 12$ ↑		**producto** Resultado de un problema de multiplicación. $3 \times 4 = 12$ ↑
pyramid A solid shape with a polygon as a base and triangular shaped faces. (page 347) 		**pirámide** Figura sólida con un polígono como base y caras de forma triangular. 

Q

English	Q	Español
quadrilateral A plane shape that has 4 sides and 4 angles. (page 353) 		**cuadrilátero** Figura que tiene 4 lados y 4 ángulos. 

Glossary/Glosario

English	Q	Español

quarter quarter = 25¢ or 25 cents (page 213)

head   tail

moneda de 25 centavos moneda de 25 centavos = 25¢ ó 25 centavos

cara   escudo

---

quarter hour One-fourth of an hour or 15 minutes. (page 393)

cuarto de hora Un cuarto de una hora ó 15 minutos.

---

quarter till (or quarter past) 15 minutes before or 15 minutes after the hour has begun. (page 393)

quarter till 11   quarter past 10

un cuarto para (o y cuarto) 15 minutos antes ó 15 minutos después de comenzar la hora.

Un cuarto para las 11   las 10 y cuarto

Glossary/Glosario

English		Español
range The difference between the greatest and least number in a set of data. (page 133)	R	**rango** La diferencia entre el número mayor y el número menor de un conjunto de datos.

English

range The difference between the greatest and least number in a set of data. (page 133)

4, 7, 10, and 2
(10 is the greatest and 2 the least)
The *range* is 8.

Español

rango La diferencia entre el número mayor y el número menor de un conjunto de datos.

4, 7, 10 y 2.
(10 es el mayor y 2 es el menor).
El *rango* es 8.

---

rectangle A plane shape with four sides and four corners.

(page 353)

rectángulo Forma con cuatro lados y cuatro esquinas.

---

rectangular prism
A solid shape with faces that are rectangles. (page 347)

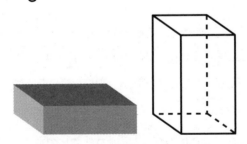

prisma rectangular Figura tridimensional con caras que son rectángulos.

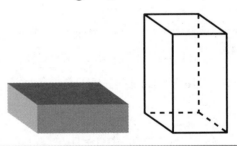

---

regroup Take apart a number to write it in a new way. (page 153)

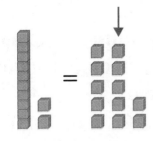

1 ten + 2 ones becomes
12 ones

reagrupar Separar un número para escribirlo de una nueva forma.

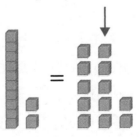

1 decena + 2 unidades se convierten en 12 unidades.

Glossary/Glosario

English	**R**	Español

related fact(s) Basic facts using the same numbers. Sometimes called a *fact family*.
(page 93)

$$4 + 1 = 5 \qquad 5 - 4 = 1$$
$$1 + 4 = 5 \qquad 5 - 1 = 4$$

operaciones relacionadas Operaciones básicas que usan los mismos números. Algunas veces se llaman *familia de operaciones*.

$$4 + 1 = 5 \qquad 5 - 4 = 1$$
$$1 + 4 = 5 \qquad 5 - 1 = 4$$

---

remainder The number that is left after one whole number is divided by another. (page 273)

residuo Número que queda después de que un número entero se divide entre otro.

---

round Change the *value* of a number to one that is easier to work with. (page 163)

24 rounded to the nearest ten is 20.

redondear Cambiar el *valor* de un número a uno con el que es más fácil trabajar.

24 redondeado a la decena más cercana es 20.

S

side One of the line segments that make up a shape. (page 359)

A pentagon has five sides.

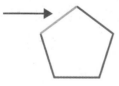

lado Uno de los segmentos de recta que componen una forma.

Un pentágono tiene cinco lados.

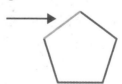

---

skip count Count objects in equal groups of two or more. (page 41)

2, 4, 6, 8, 10

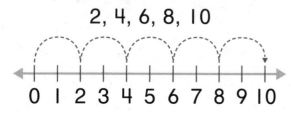

contar salteado Contar objetos en grupos iguales de dos o más.

2, 4, 6, 8, 10

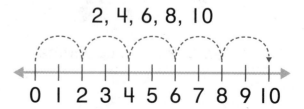

Glossary/Glosario

English	Español
solid shape A figure having the three dimensions: length, width, and height. (page 347) 	**figura sólida** Figura que tiene las tres dimensiones: largo, ancho y altura.
sphere A solid shape that has the shape of a round ball. (page 347) 	**esfera** Figura sólida que tiene la forma de pelota redonda.
square A rectangle that has four equal sides. (page 353) 	**cuadrado** Rectángulo que tiene cuatro lados iguales.
subtract (subtraction) Take away, take apart, separate, or find the difference between two sets. The opposite of *addition*. (page 83) $$5 - 5 = 0$$ 	**restar (sustracción)** Eliminar, quitar, separar o calcular la diferencia entre dos conjuntos. Lo opuesto de *adición*. $$5 - 5 = 0$$ 
subtraction sentence A math sentence that has a subtraction sign in it. (page 83) $$9 - 4 = 5$$	**enunciado de sustracción** Enunciado matemático que contiene un signo de sustracción $$9 - 5 = 4$$

Glossary/Glosario

English		Español

S

sum The answer to an addition problem. (page 53)

$$2 + 4 = 6$$

suma Resultado de un problema de adición.

$$2 + 4 = 6$$

---

survey Collect data by asking people the same questions.

(page 113)

Favorite Animal	
Dog	卌 I
Cat	卌

This survey shows people's favorite animal.

encuesta Recopilar datos al hacer las mismas preguntas a las personas.

Animal Favorito	
Perro	卌 I
Gato	卌

Esta encuesta muestra los animal favoritos.

---

symbol A letter or figure that stands for something. (page 115)

This symbol means to add.

+

símbolo Letra o figura que representa algo.

Este símbolo significa sumar.

+

T

tally mark(s) A mark used to record data collected in a survey.

(page 113)

tally marks

marca(s) de conteo Marca que se utiliza para registrar los datos recopilados en una encuesta.

marcas de conteo

Glossary/Glosario

English		Español

tens A place value of a number. (page 17)

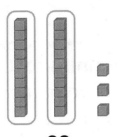

23

The 2 is in the tens place.

decenas El valor de posición de un número.

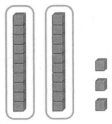

23

El 2 está en el lugar de las decenas.

---

thousand A place value of a number. (page 325)

1,253

The 1 is in the thousands place.

millar El valor de posición de un número.

1,253

El 1 está en el lugar de los millares.

3-dimensional figure See *solid shape*.

figura tridimensional. Ver la *figura sólida*.

---

trapezoid A four-sided plane shape with only two opposite sides that are the same length. (page 353)

trapecio Figura de cuatro lados con sólo dos lados opuestos que tienen la misma longitud.

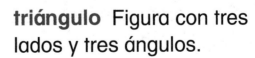

---

triangle A plane shape with three sides and three angles. (page 353)

triángulo Figura con tres lados y tres ángulos.

Glossary/Glosario

English		Español
2-dimensional figure See *plane shape*.	**T**	**figura bidimensional** Ver *figura plana*.
unit fraction Any fraction with a numerator of 1. (page 285) $$\frac{1}{2} \quad \frac{1}{3} \quad \frac{1}{4}$$	**U**	**fracción unitaria** Cualquier fracción cuyo numerador es 1. $$\frac{1}{2} \quad \frac{1}{3} \quad \frac{1}{4}$$
value How much something is worth. (page 21)	**V**	**valor** Lo que vale algo.

vertex A point on a solid shape where two or more sides (edges) meet. (page 349)

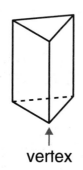

vertex

vértice Punto en una figura bidimensional o tridimensional donde se encuentran dos o más lados o aristas.

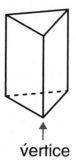

vértice

English		Español
whole The entire amount or object. (page 285)	**W**	**el todo** La cantidad total o el objeto completo.

yard A customary unit for measuring length. (page 381)

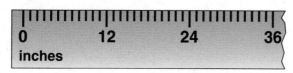

1 yard = 3 feet

Y

yarda Unidad de medida para la longitud.

1 yarda = 3 pies

Photo Credits

iv Doug Martin; **v** (br)Courtesy Dinah Zike, (others)Doug Martin; **vi** (l to r, t to b)courtesy Cheryl Avalos, courtesy William Bokesh, courtesy Patty Brown, courtesy David Chamberlain, courtesy Eppie Chung, courtesy Lisa Cirrincione, courtesy Carol Cronk, courtesy Ilene Foster, courtesy Grant Fraser; **vii** (l to r, t to b)courtesy Suzanne Freire, courtesy Beth Holguin, courtesy Donna Kopenski, courtesy Kelly Mack, courtesy Juvenal Martinez, courtesy John McGuire, courtesy Donald Price, courtesy Kasey St. James, courtesy Art Wayman, courtesy Beverly Wells, courtesy Frances Whitney; **1** Dr. Jerry M Parsons; **2** The Granger Collection, New York; **3** (t to b)Noella Ballenger/ Alamy Images, Stockdisk/Punchstock, C Squared Studios/ Getty Images, C Squared Studios/Getty Images; **5** Stephen Krasemann/NHPA; **7** CORBIS; **8** Getty Images; **9** (t to b)Richard Cummins/CORBIS, Steve Craft/Masterfile, Joseph Sohm/ChromoSohm Inc./CORBIS, Pixtal/SuperStock; **10** The McGraw-Hill Companies; **11** prettyfoto/Alamy Images; **13** Michael & Patricia Fogden/CORBIS; **15 16** Eclipse Studios; **17** Richard Hutchings; **27** (l to r t to b)Mike Houghton/StudiOhio, Mike Houghton/StudiOhio, Richard Hutchings, Mike Houghton/StudiOhio, Mike Houghton/ StudiOhio, StudiOhio, StudiOhio; **28** Mike Houghton/ StudiOhio; **29** StudiOhio; **30** (l to r)Mike Houghton/ StudiOhio, Mike Houghton/StudiOhio, C Squared Studios/ Getty Images, C Squared Studios/Getty Images; **32** David Chasey/Getty Images; **34** Steve Sant/Alamy Images; **39** Eclipse Studios; **43** Vanessa Vick/Photo Researchers; **44** (t c)LatinAmericanFolkart.com, (b)Burstein Collection/ CORBIS; **45** Mike Houghton/StudiOhio; **49** Ludovic Maisant/CORBIS; **50** (tl tr)Getty Images, (cl)Stockdisc/ PunchStock, (cr)Getty Images, (bl)Getty Images, (br)Stockdisc/PunchStock; **51** (tl)Index Stock Imagery, (tr bl br)Eclipse Studios; **52** (t)Index Stock Imagery, (b)Eclipse Studios; **59** Richard Hutchings; **60** George Doyle & Ciaran Griffin/Getty Images; **65** Getty Images; **69** Richard Hutchings; **70** (t)CORBIS, (b)Ambient Images; **71** Richard Hutchings; **72** G.K. Vikki Hart/Getty Images; **73** (t)Ed Young/CORBIS, (b)JIAN CHEN/Grant Heilman Photography; **74** (t)Inga Spence/Visuals Unlimited, (b)Richard Hutchings; **79** Denis Scott/CORBIS; **80** CORBIS; **81** (t)The McGraw-Hill Companies, (b)Eclipse Studios; **82** Eclipse Studios; **86** PhotoEdit; **87** Richard Hutchings; **88** (t)Ambient Images, (b)Ambient Images Inc./ Alamy Images; **90** (t)Brand X Pictures/PunchStock, (b)PhotoLink/Getty Images; **93 99** Richard Hutchings; **101** Eclipse Studios; **103** (t)Michael Newman/PhotoEdit, (b)David Frazier/PhotoEdit; **104** (t)Fabio Cardoso/zefa/ CORBIS, (b)Purestock/PunchStock; **108** C Squared Studios/Getty Images; **109** Rob Walls/Alamy Images; **111** (tl)Klaus Hackenberg/zefa/CORBIS, (others)Eclipse Studios; **112** (t)Klaus Hackenberg/zefa/CORBIS, (b)Eclipse Studios; **113** Richard Hutchings; **115** G.K. Vikki Hart/Getty Images; **119** Getty Images; **120** (t)James Urbach/SuperStock, (b)Jeremy Woodhouse/Getty Images; **126** Richard Price/ Getty Images; **127** (l)Richard Hutchings, (r)Eclipse Studios; **131** Grant Faint/Getty Images; **135** Richard Hutchings; **137** (t)F. Schussler/PhotoLink/Getty Images, (b)Rhoda Sidney/ PhotoEdit; **138** CORBIS; **143** John Eastcott/Minden Pictures; **145 146** Eclipse Studios; **150** Bill Aron/PhotoEdit; **151** Masterfile; **152** (t to b)2006 Photos To Go, 2006 Photos To Go, Getty Images, The McGraw-Hill Companies; **163 165** Richard Hutchings; **166** (t)John Blair/Alamy Images, (b)Robert Maier/Animals Animals; **167** Laura Dwight/PhotoEdit; **169** (t)CORBIS, (b)Ericka McConnell/ Taxi/Getty Images; **170** (t)Mike Powell/Getty Images, (b)Colin Barker/Getty Images; **175** CORBIS; **177 178** Eclipse Studios; **179** Richard Hutchings; **180 182** CORBIS; **188** Mike Houghton/StudiOhio; **195** Richard Hutchings; **196** (t)Rick Doyle/CORBIS, (b)Richard Koek /Getty Images; **197** Richard Hutchings; **207** Mike Houghton/StudiOhio; **209** (t)Michael Houghton/StudiOhio, (b)Eclipse Studios; **210** Eclipse Studios; **213** (t)Brand X Pictures/PunchStock, (c)Getty Images, (b)CORBIS; **214** (t)Squared Studios/Getty Images, (c)The McGraw-Hill Companies, (b)CORBIS; **215** 2006 Photos To Go; **216** (t to b)Comstock Images/Alamy Images, 2006 Photos To Go, Getty Images, Getty Images; **217** Siede Preis/Getty Images; **219** (l to r t to b)Michael Houghton/StudiOhio, The McGraw-Hill Companies, StudiOhio, StudiOhio, StudiOhio, PhotoLink/Getty Images; **223 225 226 227** Michael Houghton/StudiOhio; **229** (tl)Michael Houghton/StudiOhio, (tr)StudiOhio, (c)C Squared Studios/Getty Images, (b)Getty Images; **230** (l to r t to b)Michael Houghton/StudiOhio, Getty Images, Getty Images, Getty Images, The McGraw-Hill Companies; **231** Michael Houghton/StudiOhio; **233** StudiOhio; **237** Michael Newman/PhotoEdit; **238** (t)Getty Images, (b)C Squared Studios/Getty Images; **239** (t)Rich Pedroncelli/AP Images, (b)Jason Hunt/AP Images; **240** (bkgd)Getty Images, (l to r t to b)Getty Images, Getty Images, Jacqueline Larma/ AP Images, Bettmann/CORBIS; **241** Michael Houghton/ StudiOhio; **242** (l)Michael Houghton/StudiOhio, (r)Siede Preis/Getty Images; **245** Rob Kearney/Getty Images; **246** C Squared Studios/Getty Images; **247** (t)Richard Hutchings, (others)Eclipse Studios; **248** Eclipse Studios; **251** Richard Hutchings; **252** (tl)The McGraw-Hill Companies, (tr)2006 Photos To Go, (c)Jupiterimages, (b)StudiOhio; **260** C Squared Studios/Getty Images; **264** (t)Greg Vaughn/Alamy Images, (b)Greg Ochocki/Photo Researchers; **265** (t)PhotoLink/Getty Images, (b)The McGraw-Hill Companies; **270** C Squared Studios/Getty Images; **271** Richard Hutchings; **272** (t to b)The McGraw-Hill Companies, Getty Images, Siede Preis/Getty Images, Ryan McVay/Getty Images; **273** Richard Hutchings; **275** (t)Bettmann/CORBIS, (b)Blend Images/Getty Images; **276** Bettmann/CORBIS; **281** Mike Houghton/StudiOhio; **283** (l)Eclipse Studios, (tr)Getty Images, (cr br)Eclipse Studios; **284** Eclipse Studios; **286** StudiOhio; **291** Richard Hutchings; **292** Penny Adams/SuperStock; **299** (tl tr)Richard Hutchings, (cl)The McGraw-Hill Companies, (c cr)StudiOhio, (bl)The McGraw-Hill Companies, (bc br)Jupiterimages; **301** (t)The McGraw-Hill Companies, (b)StudiOhio; **303** Eclipse Studios; **304** The McGraw-Hill Companies; **306** (t)Bruce Dale/Getty Images, (b)Wally Bauman/Alamy Images; **311** David Tipling/Getty Images; **313 314** Eclipse Studios; **317** StudiOhio; **318** Craig Lovell/CORBIS; **329** Eclipse Studios; **338** (t)Lothar Lenz/zefa/CORBIS, (b)Digital Vision/Getty Images; **343** Alan Schein Photography/CORBIS; **344** (cw from top)Getty Images, McGraw-Hill Companies, Steve Cole/Getty Images, Ryan McVay/Getty Images, The McGraw-Hill Companies, Ryan McVay/Getty Images, Brand X/PunchStock, 2006 Photos To Go, Getty Images, Punchstock/Getty Images; **345 346** Eclipse Studios; **337** (t)Bettmann/CORBIS, (c)C Squared Studios/Getty Images, (bl)TRBfoto/Getty Images, (br)Siede Preis/Getty Images; **347** (l to r)The McGraw-Hill Companies, The McGraw-Hill Companies, The McGraw-Hill Companies, The McGraw-Hill Companies, The McGraw-Hill Companies, Stockbyte/

PictureQuest, The McGraw-Hill Companies, The McGraw-Hill Companies, C Squares Studios/Getty Images, Siede Preis/Getty Images, The McGraw-Hill Companies, Getty Images, The McGraw-Hill Companies, Craig Lovell/CORBIS, Alamy Images, The McGraw-Hill Companies, Jupiterimages, Punchstock/Getty Images, Getty Images, 2006 Photos To Go, Getty Images, The McGraw-Hill Companies; **350** (l to r t to b)The McGraw-Hill Companies, The McGraw-Hill Companies, Ryan McVay/Getty Images, Stockdisc/PunchStock, 2006 Photos To Go, Punchstock/Getty Images, Getty Images, Jupiterimages, Brand X/PunchStock/Getty Images, The McGraw-Hill Companies, Getty Images, Alamy Images, Micahel Matisse/Getty Images, The McGraw-Hill Companies, The McGraw-Hill Companies, Siede Preis/Getty Images, Alamy Images, Getty Images; **357** (l to r t to b)The McGraw-Hill Companies, Jupiterimages, Getty Images, CORBIS, 2006 Photos To Go, Jupiterimages, Getty Images, Burke/Triolo Productions/Getty Images, 2006 Photos To Go, The McGraw-Hill Companies, Punchstock/Getty Images, The McGraw-Hill Companies, Stockbyte/PictureQuest, Burke/Triolo/Brand X/Jupiterimages, The McGraw-Hill Companies, The McGraw-Hill Companies, The McGraw-Hill Companies; **358** Getty Images; **360** (tl)Arthur S. Aubry/Getty Images, (tcl tr c cl cr br)Getty Images, (tc bc)McGraw-Hill Companies, (bl)Sarah Murray/Masterfile; **361** (tl)StudiOhio, (tr)Richard Hutchings, (bl br)StudiOhio; **362** (tl tr)Alamy Images, (bl)Raimund Koch/Getty Images, (br)McGraw-Hill Companies; **363** Richard Hutchings; **364** Ken Lucas/Visuals Unlimited; **365** Michael Newman/PhotoEdit; **367** (t)Alamy Images, (c)Jim Zuckerman/CORBIS, (b)Getty Images; **368** (t)Catherine Ledner/Getty Images, (b)Masterfile; **369** (l to r)The McGraw-Hill Companies, 2006 Photos To Go, The McGraw-Hill Companies, C Squares Studios/Getty Images, Punchstock/Getty Images, The McGraw-Hill Companies; **370** (tl)Michael Houghton/StudiOhio, (tr c)Getty Image, (b)The McGraw-Hill Companies; **371** (l to r)2006 Photos To Go, The McGraw-Hill Companies, Getty Images, The McGraw-Hill Companies; **373** Chris Windsor/Getty Images; **375 376** Eclipse Studios; **377** (tl b)McGraw-Hill Companies, (tr)Richard Hutching, (c)Getty Images; **378** (t)Stockbyte/PictureQuest, (c)Jupiterimages, (b)The McGraw-Hill Companies; **379** (tl tr)Richard Hutchings, (c)Alamy Images,(b)C Squared Studios/Getty Images; **380** (t to b)Burke/Triolo/Brand X Pictures/Jupiterimages, StudiOhio, The McGraw-Hill Companies, The McGraw-Hill Companies, PhotoLink/Getty Images, C Squared Studios/Getty Images; **381** (t)Richard Hutchings, (c)McGraw-Hill Companies, (b)Andy Crawford/Getty Images; **382** (t to b)Brian Klutch/Getty Images, Jupiterimages, Peter M. Fisher/CORBIS, The McGraw-Hill Companies; **384** (t)Stockdisc/PunchStock, (c)The McGraw-Hill Companies, (b)Getty Images; **387** (t)StudiOhio, (c)Thomas Northcut/Getty Images, (b)Brand X/Punchstock/Getty Images; **388** (t to b)McGraw-Hill Companies, Getty Images, Getty Images, The McGraw-Hill Companies, PhotoLink/Getty Images, C Squared Studios/Getty Images, Michael Houghton/StudiOhio; **389** (t)Richard Hutchings, (c)PhotoLink/Getty Images, (b)Brian Klutch/Getty Images; **390** Jupiterimages; **391** (t to b)The McGraw-Hill Companies, The McGraw-Hill Companies, CORBIS, Najlah Feanny/CORBIS, Jupiterimages, Jeffery w. Myers/CORBIS; **395** Eclipse Studios; **398** (tl)Burke/Triolo Productions/Getty Images, (tr)C Squared Studios/Getty Images, (bl)G.K. Vikki Hart/Getty Images, (br)Getty Images; **399** (t to b)Getty Images, CORBIS, CORBIS, Siede Preis/Getty Images, Jupiterimages; **400** (t)CORBIS, (c)Ryan McVay/Getty Images, (b)AP Images; **401** (tl)Michael Newman/PhotoEdit, (tr)Michelle D. Bridwell/PhotoEdit, (bl)David Young-Wolff/PhotoEdit, (br)Peter Griffin/Alamy Images; **402** (l to r t to b)Susan Van Etten/PhotoEdit, Blend Images/SuperStock, Getty Images, Kim Karpeles/Alamy Images, Tom McCarthy/PhotoEdit, 2006 Photos To Go; **403** (t)Shalom Ormsby/Getty Images, (b)Nicholas Prior/Stone/Getty Images; **405** (t to b)PhotoLink/Getty Images, Najlah Feanny/CORBIS, Peter M. Fisher/CORBIS, Andy Crawford/Getty Images, Burke/Triolo/Brand X Pictures/Jupiterimages, CORBIS; **406** (t)S. Alden/Getty Images, (b)Albert Normandin/Masterfile; **408** The McGraw-Hill Companies; **409** WireImageStock/Masterfile; **410** C Squared Studios/Getty Images; **411 412** Eclipse Studios; **414** Getty Images; **420** Gunter Marx Photography/CORBIS; **429** Mark Hall/Getty Images; **431** (t)Erin Hogan/Getty Images, (b)Joe Drivas/Getty Images; **432** Bob Sciarrino/Star Ledger/CORBIS; **435** The McGraw-Hill Companies; **437** Steve Bloom/Steve Bloom Images; **438** PhotoLink/Getty Images; **439 440** Eclipse Studios; **448** Bettman/CORBIS; **452** (l to r)The McGraw-Hill Companies, The McGraw-Hill Companies, Ryan McVay/Getty Images, Getty Images, Steve Cole/Getty Images, The McGraw-Hill Companies; **455** Bob Daemmrich/PhotoEdit; **457** Eclipse Studios; **459** (t)CORBIS, (b)Mitch Hrdlicka/Getty Images; **460** (tl)CORBIS, (tr)Mark E. Gibson/CORBIS, (b)CORBIS; **465 466** Tim Fuller; **469** C Squared Studios/Getty Images; **471** (t to b)Richard Hutchings, Judith Collins/Alamy Images, Dave King, Andy Crawford, Steve Gorton/Getty Images, Getty Images; **472** (t to b)C Squared Studios/Getty Images, CORBIS, John A. Rizzo/Getty Images, The McGraw-Hill Companies, foodfolio/Alamy Images; **473** (tl tr)The McGraw-Hill Companies, (c)Getty Images, (bl)Jacques Cornell/The McGraw-Hill Companies, (br)Brand X Pictures/Alamy Images; **474** (t to b)The McGraw-Hill Companies, Phil Degginger/Alamy Images, Lynx/Iconotec.com/Alamy Images, The McGraw-Hill Companies; **475** (tl tr)StudiOhio, (c)Brand X Pictures/PunchStock, (bl)The McGraw-Hill Companies, (br)CORBIS; **476** (t to b)Sky Bonillo/PhotoEdit, Nikreates/Alamy Images, Getty Images, Getty Images, Sam Toren/Alamy Images, StudiOhio; **477** (tl tr cl)StudiOhio, (cr)G.K. Vikki Hart/Getty Images, (bl)The McGraw-Hill Companies, (bc br)Getty Images; **478** (t to b)Getty Images, C Squared Studios/Getty Images, CORBIS, Simon Battensby/Getty Images, The McGraw-Hill Companies; **R8** Michael Houghton/StudiOhio; **R13** (t)Getty Images, (c)Ryan McVay/Getty Images, (b)Getty Images; **R14** C Squared Studios/Getty Images.

Art Credits

McGraw-Hill would like to acknowledge the artists and agencies who contributed to illustrating this program: Cover Jim Talbot represented by Mendola Artists; Fian Arroyo; 3DI, Articulate Graphics, Bob Depew, John Hom, Studio Liddell, and Bob Wakelin represented by AA Reps. Inc.

Name _____

Subtract from 14 or less (Use with Chapter 8)

1.
$$\begin{array}{r}14\\-\ 5\\\hline\end{array}\qquad\begin{array}{r}13\\-\ 6\\\hline\end{array}\qquad\begin{array}{r}14\\-\ 7\\\hline\end{array}\qquad\begin{array}{r}14\\-\ 9\\\hline\end{array}\qquad\begin{array}{r}14\\-\ 8\\\hline\end{array}\qquad\begin{array}{r}11\\-\ 2\\\hline\end{array}$$

2.
$$\begin{array}{r}12\\-\ 8\\\hline\end{array}\qquad\begin{array}{r}12\\-\ 7\\\hline\end{array}\qquad\begin{array}{r}12\\-\ 5\\\hline\end{array}\qquad\begin{array}{r}13\\-\ 9\\\hline\end{array}\qquad\begin{array}{r}14\\-\ 7\\\hline\end{array}\qquad\begin{array}{r}13\\-\ 8\\\hline\end{array}$$

3.
$$\begin{array}{r}14\\-\ 8\\\hline\end{array}\qquad\begin{array}{r}11\\-\ 5\\\hline\end{array}\qquad\begin{array}{r}14\\-\ 5\\\hline\end{array}\qquad\begin{array}{r}14\\-\ 6\\\hline\end{array}\qquad\begin{array}{r}13\\-\ 8\\\hline\end{array}\qquad\begin{array}{r}12\\-\ 9\\\hline\end{array}$$

- -

Name _____

Facts to 18 (Use with Chapter 9)

1.
$$\begin{array}{r}9\\+\ 9\\\hline\end{array}\qquad\begin{array}{r}9\\+\ 2\\\hline\end{array}\qquad\begin{array}{r}8\\+\ 4\\\hline\end{array}\qquad\begin{array}{r}5\\+\ 6\\\hline\end{array}\qquad\begin{array}{r}7\\+\ 9\\\hline\end{array}\qquad\begin{array}{r}6\\+\ 4\\\hline\end{array}$$

2.
$$\begin{array}{r}7\\+\ 8\\\hline\end{array}\qquad\begin{array}{r}7\\+\ 6\\\hline\end{array}\qquad\begin{array}{r}6\\+\ 6\\\hline\end{array}\qquad\begin{array}{r}6\\+\ 9\\\hline\end{array}\qquad\begin{array}{r}4\\+\ 9\\\hline\end{array}\qquad\begin{array}{r}9\\+\ 8\\\hline\end{array}$$

3.
$$\begin{array}{r}9\\+\ 5\\\hline\end{array}\qquad\begin{array}{r}9\\+\ 3\\\hline\end{array}\qquad\begin{array}{r}6\\+\ 8\\\hline\end{array}\qquad\begin{array}{r}2\\+\ 6\\\hline\end{array}\qquad\begin{array}{r}8\\+\ 8\\\hline\end{array}\qquad\begin{array}{r}7\\+\ 2\\\hline\end{array}$$

Subtract from 14 or less (Use with Chapter 8)

4.
$$\begin{array}{r} 14 \\ -\ 6 \\ \hline \end{array} \qquad \begin{array}{r} 11 \\ -\ 3 \\ \hline \end{array} \qquad \begin{array}{r} 14 \\ -\ 7 \\ \hline \end{array} \qquad \begin{array}{r} 14 \\ -\ 5 \\ \hline \end{array} \qquad \begin{array}{r} 11 \\ -\ 9 \\ \hline \end{array} \qquad \begin{array}{r} 14 \\ -\ 8 \\ \hline \end{array}$$

5.
$$\begin{array}{r} 14 \\ -\ 9 \\ \hline \end{array} \qquad \begin{array}{r} 13 \\ -\ 4 \\ \hline \end{array} \qquad \begin{array}{r} 14 \\ -\ 5 \\ \hline \end{array} \qquad \begin{array}{r} 11 \\ -\ 7 \\ \hline \end{array} \qquad \begin{array}{r} 14 \\ -\ 8 \\ \hline \end{array} \qquad \begin{array}{r} 13 \\ -\ 7 \\ \hline \end{array}$$

6.
$$\begin{array}{r} 14 \\ -\ 7 \\ \hline \end{array} \qquad \begin{array}{r} 14 \\ -\ 6 \\ \hline \end{array} \qquad \begin{array}{r} 12 \\ -\ 8 \\ \hline \end{array} \qquad \begin{array}{r} 13 \\ -\ 5 \\ \hline \end{array} \qquad \begin{array}{r} 14 \\ -\ 9 \\ \hline \end{array} \qquad \begin{array}{r} 12 \\ -\ 4 \\ \hline \end{array}$$

- -

Facts to 18 (Use with Chapter 9)

4.
$$\begin{array}{r} 5 \\ +\ 8 \\ \hline \end{array} \qquad \begin{array}{r} 7 \\ +\ 4 \\ \hline \end{array} \qquad \begin{array}{r} 5 \\ +\ 9 \\ \hline \end{array} \qquad \begin{array}{r} 8 \\ +\ 9 \\ \hline \end{array} \qquad \begin{array}{r} 6 \\ +\ 5 \\ \hline \end{array} \qquad \begin{array}{r} 7 \\ +\ 3 \\ \hline \end{array}$$

5.
$$\begin{array}{r} 9 \\ +\ 4 \\ \hline \end{array} \qquad \begin{array}{r} 5 \\ +\ 7 \\ \hline \end{array} \qquad \begin{array}{r} 5 \\ +\ 4 \\ \hline \end{array} \qquad \begin{array}{r} 7 \\ +\ 7 \\ \hline \end{array} \qquad \begin{array}{r} 6 \\ +\ 7 \\ \hline \end{array} \qquad \begin{array}{r} 6 \\ +\ 6 \\ \hline \end{array}$$

6.
$$\begin{array}{r} 8 \\ +\ 7 \\ \hline \end{array} \qquad \begin{array}{r} 8 \\ +\ 2 \\ \hline \end{array} \qquad \begin{array}{r} 7 \\ +\ 5 \\ \hline \end{array} \qquad \begin{array}{r} 9 \\ +\ 6 \\ \hline \end{array} \qquad \begin{array}{r} 8 \\ +\ 6 \\ \hline \end{array} \qquad \begin{array}{r} 9 \\ +\ 7 \\ \hline \end{array}$$

Facts Practice

Name _____

Subtract from 18 or less (Use with Chapter 9)

1.
$$\begin{array}{r} 15 \\ -\ 8 \\ \hline \end{array}$$
$$\begin{array}{r} 12 \\ -\ 9 \\ \hline \end{array}$$
$$\begin{array}{r} 13 \\ -\ 6 \\ \hline \end{array}$$
$$\begin{array}{r} 18 \\ -\ 9 \\ \hline \end{array}$$
$$\begin{array}{r} 13 \\ -\ 4 \\ \hline \end{array}$$
$$\begin{array}{r} 12 \\ -\ 7 \\ \hline \end{array}$$

2.
$$\begin{array}{r} 12 \\ -\ 4 \\ \hline \end{array}$$
$$\begin{array}{r} 12 \\ -\ 5 \\ \hline \end{array}$$
$$\begin{array}{r} 18 \\ -\ 9 \\ \hline \end{array}$$
$$\begin{array}{r} 17 \\ -\ 9 \\ \hline \end{array}$$
$$\begin{array}{r} 15 \\ -\ 9 \\ \hline \end{array}$$
$$\begin{array}{r} 12 \\ -\ 6 \\ \hline \end{array}$$

3.
$$\begin{array}{r} 12 \\ -\ 8 \\ \hline \end{array}$$
$$\begin{array}{r} 16 \\ -\ 7 \\ \hline \end{array}$$
$$\begin{array}{r} 17 \\ -\ 8 \\ \hline \end{array}$$
$$\begin{array}{r} 13 \\ -\ 5 \\ \hline \end{array}$$
$$\begin{array}{r} 16 \\ -\ 9 \\ \hline \end{array}$$
$$\begin{array}{r} 16 \\ -\ 8 \\ \hline \end{array}$$

Name _____

Multiply by 2 (Use with Chapter 10)

1.
$$\begin{array}{r} 2 \\ \times\ 0 \\ \hline \end{array}$$
$$\begin{array}{r} 2 \\ \times\ 4 \\ \hline \end{array}$$
$$\begin{array}{r} 9 \\ \times\ 2 \\ \hline \end{array}$$
$$\begin{array}{r} 5 \\ \times\ 2 \\ \hline \end{array}$$
$$\begin{array}{r} 2 \\ \times\ 9 \\ \hline \end{array}$$
$$\begin{array}{r} 7 \\ \times\ 2 \\ \hline \end{array}$$

2.
$$\begin{array}{r} 2 \\ \times\ 7 \\ \hline \end{array}$$
$$\begin{array}{r} 6 \\ \times\ 2 \\ \hline \end{array}$$
$$\begin{array}{r} 2 \\ \times\ 2 \\ \hline \end{array}$$
$$\begin{array}{r} 2 \\ \times\ 6 \\ \hline \end{array}$$
$$\begin{array}{r} 1 \\ \times\ 2 \\ \hline \end{array}$$
$$\begin{array}{r} 2 \\ \times\ 8 \\ \hline \end{array}$$

3.
$$\begin{array}{r} 2 \\ \times\ 3 \\ \hline \end{array}$$
$$\begin{array}{r} 3 \\ \times\ 2 \\ \hline \end{array}$$
$$\begin{array}{r} 4 \\ \times\ 2 \\ \hline \end{array}$$
$$\begin{array}{r} 8 \\ \times\ 2 \\ \hline \end{array}$$
$$\begin{array}{r} 2 \\ \times\ 1 \\ \hline \end{array}$$
$$\begin{array}{r} 2 \\ \times\ 5 \\ \hline \end{array}$$

Subtract from 18 or less (Use with Chapter 9)

4.
18	13	15	16	17	14
− 9	− 8	− 9	− 7	− 9	− 8

5.
15	14	13	14	14	16
− 6	− 7	− 7	− 9	− 5	− 8

6.
17	15	14	16	13	18
− 8	− 8	− 6	− 9	− 9	− 9

- -

Name _____

Multiply by 2 (Use with Chapter 10)

4.
2	4	9	2	2	5
× 6	× 2	× 2	× 8	× 3	× 2

5.
8	2	2	2	6	3
× 2	× 0	× 1	× 7	× 2	× 2

6.
2	7	2	1	2	2
× 2	× 2	× 5	× 2	× 4	× 9

Facts Practice

Name _____

Related Facts to 12 (Use with Chapter 11)

1.
| 8
+ 3 | 11
− 3 | 12
− 5 | 7
+ 5 | 5
+ 6 | 11
− 6 |

2.
| 11
− 4 | 7
+ 4 | 9
+ 2 | 11
− 2 | 10
− 6 | 4
+ 6 |

3.
| 11
− 8 | 3
+ 8 | 12
− 3 | 9
+ 3 | 12
− 4 | 8
+ 4 |

- -

Name _____

Multiply by 5 (Use with Chapter 12)

1.
| 5
× 1 | 5
× 4 | 3
× 5 | 2
× 5 | 7
× 5 | 4
× 5 |

2.
| 5
× 6 | 6
× 5 | 5
× 7 | 5
× 3 | 1
× 5 | 8
× 5 |

3.
| 5
× 9 | 5
× 2 | 4
× 5 | 5
× 0 | 5
× 8 | 5
× 5 |

Related Facts to 12 (Use with Chapter 11)

4.

| $\begin{array}{r} 12 \\ -\ 6 \\ \hline \end{array}$ | $\begin{array}{r} 6 \\ +\ 6 \\ \hline \end{array}$ | $\begin{array}{r} 10 \\ -\ 3 \\ \hline \end{array}$ | $\begin{array}{r} 7 \\ +\ 3 \\ \hline \end{array}$ | $\begin{array}{r} 10 \\ -\ 8 \\ \hline \end{array}$ | $\begin{array}{r} 2 \\ +\ 8 \\ \hline \end{array}$ |

5.

| $\begin{array}{r} 2 \\ +\ 9 \\ \hline \end{array}$ | $\begin{array}{r} 11 \\ -\ 9 \\ \hline \end{array}$ | $\begin{array}{r} 12 \\ -\ 9 \\ \hline \end{array}$ | $\begin{array}{r} 3 \\ +\ 9 \\ \hline \end{array}$ | $\begin{array}{r} 12 \\ -\ 7 \\ \hline \end{array}$ | $\begin{array}{r} 5 \\ +\ 7 \\ \hline \end{array}$ |

6.

| $\begin{array}{r} 4 \\ +\ 7 \\ \hline \end{array}$ | $\begin{array}{r} 11 \\ -\ 7 \\ \hline \end{array}$ | $\begin{array}{r} 12 \\ -\ 8 \\ \hline \end{array}$ | $\begin{array}{r} 4 \\ +\ 8 \\ \hline \end{array}$ | $\begin{array}{r} 6 \\ +\ 5 \\ \hline \end{array}$ | $\begin{array}{r} 11 \\ -\ 5 \\ \hline \end{array}$ |

- -

Multiply by 5 (Use with Chapter 12)

4.

| $\begin{array}{r} 5 \\ \times\ 9 \\ \hline \end{array}$ | $\begin{array}{r} 5 \\ \times\ 0 \\ \hline \end{array}$ | $\begin{array}{r} 2 \\ \times\ 5 \\ \hline \end{array}$ | $\begin{array}{r} 1 \\ \times\ 5 \\ \hline \end{array}$ | $\begin{array}{r} 3 \\ \times\ 5 \\ \hline \end{array}$ | $\begin{array}{r} 5 \\ \times\ 6 \\ \hline \end{array}$ |

5.

| $\begin{array}{r} 4 \\ \times\ 5 \\ \hline \end{array}$ | $\begin{array}{r} 5 \\ \times\ 2 \\ \hline \end{array}$ | $\begin{array}{r} 5 \\ \times\ 7 \\ \hline \end{array}$ | $\begin{array}{r} 8 \\ \times\ 5 \\ \hline \end{array}$ | $\begin{array}{r} 5 \\ \times\ 5 \\ \hline \end{array}$ | $\begin{array}{r} 9 \\ \times\ 5 \\ \hline \end{array}$ |

6.

| $\begin{array}{r} 5 \\ \times\ 8 \\ \hline \end{array}$ | $\begin{array}{r} 7 \\ \times\ 5 \\ \hline \end{array}$ | $\begin{array}{r} 1 \\ \times\ 5 \\ \hline \end{array}$ | $\begin{array}{r} 5 \\ \times\ 3 \\ \hline \end{array}$ | $\begin{array}{r} 5 \\ \times\ 4 \\ \hline \end{array}$ | $\begin{array}{r} 8 \\ \times\ 5 \\ \hline \end{array}$ |

Facts Practice

Name _____

Related Facts to 18 (Use with Chapter 13)

1.	18 − 9	9 + 9	17 − 9	9 + 8	16 − 8	8 + 8
2.	14 − 8	8 + 6	7 + 8	15 − 7	8 + 6	14 − 8
3.	9 + 6	15 − 9	15 − 6	9 + 6	15 − 8	7 + 8

- ✂

Name _____

Multiply by 10 (Use with Chapter 14)

1.	10 × 9	4 ×10	10 × 7	5 ×10	1 ×10	2 ×10
2.	10 × 6	10 × 2	9 ×10	10 × 0	10 × 5	3 ×10
3.	10 × 4	10 × 3	6 ×10	10 × 1	10 × 8	7 ×10

Facts Practice

Copyright © Macmillan/McGraw-Hill, a division of The McGraw-Hill Companies, Inc.

Related Facts to 18 (Use with Chapter 13)

4.

| 13
− 6 | 6
+ 7 | 14
− 8 | 6
+ 8 | 13
− 5 | 5
+ 8 |

5.

| 14
− 7 | 7
+ 7 | 11
− 7 | 4
+ 7 | 15
− 8 | 8
+ 7 |

6.

| 11
− 6 | 5
+ 6 | 9
+ 9 | 18
− 9 | 16
− 8 | 8
+ 8 |

Multiply by 10 (Use with Chapter 14)

4.

| 10
× 9 | 2
×10 | 3
×10 | 10
× 4 | 10
× 7 | 10
× 1 |

5.

| 10
× 0 | 7
×10 | 10
× 8 | 4
×10 | 10
× 1 | 10
× 6 |

6.

| 6
×10 | 5
×10 | 10
× 2 | 9
×10 | 10
× 5 | 8
×10 |

Facts Practice

WorkMat 1

WorkMat 1: Ten–Frame

WorkMat 2: Ten–Frames

Part

Part

Whole

WorkMat 3: Part–Part–Whole

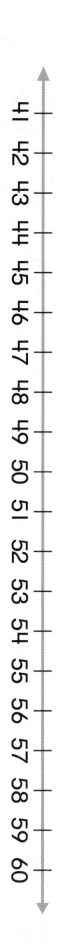

0 1 2 3 4 5 6 7 8 9 10 11 12 13 14 15 16 17 18 19 20

21 22 23 24 25 26 27 28 29 30 31 32 33 34 35 36 37 38 39 40

41 42 43 44 45 46 47 48 49 50 51 52 53 54 55 56 57 58 59 60

WorkMat 4: Number Lines

WorkMat 5

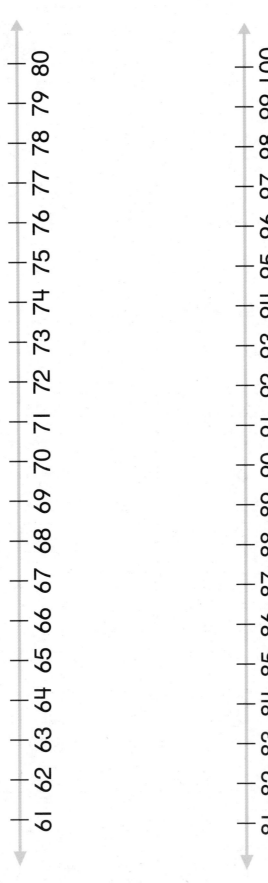

61 62 63 64 65 66 67 68 69 70 71 72 73 74 75 76 77 78 79 80

81 82 83 84 85 86 87 88 89 90 91 92 93 94 95 96 97 98 99 100

WorkMat 5: Number Lines

Tens	Ones

WorkMat 6: Tens and Ones Chart

Hundreds	Tens	Ones

WorkMat 7: Hundreds, Tens, and Ones Chart

Thousands	Hundreds	Tens	Ones

WorkMat 8

WorkMat 8: Thousands, Hundreds, Tens, and Ones Chart